AND NOW A FEW WORDS FROM ME

ADVERTISING'S LEADING CRITIC LAYS DOWN THE LAW, ONCE AND FOR ALL

BOB GARFIELD

McGraw-Hill

New York   Chicago   San Francisco   Lisbon   London   Madrid   Mexico City
Milan   New Delhi   San Juan   Seoul   Singapore   Sydney   Toronto

The *McGraw·Hill* Companies

Library of Congress Cataloging-in-Publication Data

Garfield, Bob.
    And now a few words from me : advertising's leading critic lays down the law,
once and for all / Bob Garfield.
        p.   cm.
    Includes index.
    ISBN 0-07-140316-7 (hardcover) — ISBN 0-07-144122-0 (paperback)
    1. Advertising.   2. Marketing.   I. Title.

HF5823 .G27   2003
659.1—dc21   2002031249

"Into the Valley" Words and music by Richard Jobson and William Stuart Adamson.
© 1980 EMI Virgin Music Ltd. All rights in the United States and Canada controlled and
administered by EMI Virgin Music, Inc. All rights reserved. International copyright
secured. Used by permission.
Deadly Persuasion: Why Women and Girls Must Fight the Addictive Power of Advertising
by Jean Kilbourne. Copyright © 1999 by Jean Kilbourne. Reprinted with permission of
The Free Press, an imprint of Simon & Schuster Trade Publishing Group.

1 2 3 4 5 6 7 8 9 0   LBM/LBM   3 2 1 0 9 8 7 6 5 4

ISBN 0-07-140316-7 (hardcover)
ISBN 0-07-144122-0 (paperback)

Interior design by Steve Straus
Cover design by Brian Boucher
Cover photo by Chris Cassidy

For my daughters, Katie, Allie, and Ida Rose

CONTENTS

INTRODUCTION

The Ten Commandments of Advertising, Brought to You by God

All right, maybe not exactly from God, directly. The King of Kings is extremely tied up at the moment creating all light and life in the universe and bestowing infinite love and finding new ways to drown Bangladeshis and considering desperate prayers from sports fans and the hung over. Though He is almighty and a phenomenal multitasker, you don't get to be Supreme Being without knowing when to delegate.

That's where I come in.

In the absence of stone tablets or explicit scriptural instruction for correctly promoting products and services to consumers via the mass media, God has left it for certain servants on earth to codify what certainly would be His commandments if marketing were higher on the heavenly agenda. It is an awesome responsibility, which I am proud and humbled to take on.

And, really, if not me, who?

For more than twenty years I have used my column first in *USA Today* and since 1985 in *Advertising Age* to evaluate, deconstruct,

explain, interpret, upbraid, and—more often than you'd expect—
praise advertising from all over the world. I have vetted advertising
for strategy, relevance, production values, originality, communications
ingenuity, humor, narrative, emotion, psychology, cinematography,
music, photo composition, editing, direction, lighting, acting, writing, typography, grammar, honesty, offensiveness, and, as befits my
role as divine surrogate, morality.

The last consideration has consumed far more time than I
would have preferred, thanks to a cultural sea change in the industry over the last decade, which has seen the imperative of getting
attention override such tired old values as the Golden Rule. You will
be hearing more about this later (Chapter 6, "Be My Guest"), but for
now let's just say that the relentlessly encroaching forces of barbarism
threaten advertising civilization. If only for that reason (but, of
course, also for many others), this book will illuminate the way.

Yes, my child, the one true path.

But I digress. Back to me, because there is something else you
need to know that qualifies me for this solemn mission: I am never
wrong. Anyway, hardly ever. Over seventeen years of writing "Ad
Review," with well in excess of a thousand ads subjected to my piti-
less scrutiny, I've really blown the call only eleven or twelve times.
(Ask me sometime about Saturn and Reebok's UBU. Like . . . ouch.)
In baseball terms that's hitting .988. Considering that I write about
campaigns that have just broken, or not broken yet, that batting average at predicting success or failure is pretty phenomenal. In fact, in
all modesty, it is entirely phenomenal—a record I attribute to two
factors:

Number one, advertising, at its essence, is not a complicated
enterprise. Surely it is a business with many complications, but fundamentally it is about nothing more complex than communicating a
selling idea to a prospective customer. If some fast-talking goof on
the Atlantic City boardwalk can do this with a vegetable peeler, the

greatest minds in marketing should be able to pull it off with millions of dollars and a vast media world at their disposal. Yet so often they fail, for reasons that jump plainly from the TV screen to any non-nitwit willing to give them a moment's honest thought.

Factor two: I'm not a nitwit.

Nor are advertising professionals . . . you know, for the most part. These are often very smart people—smart people doing the same stupid things, day after day. This book will cite those mistakes chapter and verse until you are not only snorting with contempt but holding your head and groaning in incredulity. Yes, you will reflect on the mind-boggling blunders of the handsomely compensated advertising elite and actually make pained noises. But why is that? Why is it that what I see so plainly, and what you see so plainly, is so elusive to them?

SVENGALIS? YEAH, RIGHT

The first answer is perspective. It's my belief (based on no inside information beyond the testimony of my own eyes) that agencies and clients alike get so caught up in the process of realizing their strategic and creative visions—and so romanticizing and mystifying the so-called creative process—that they lose sight altogether of how their output is seen by the outside world. Myopia by immersion, I've heard this called, and nowhere is the phenomenon more apparent than advertising. The worst ads I've seen in my criticism career haven't been detected by my ground radar flying close to the deck under the cover of darkness; they've come to me by FedEx attached to press releases trumpeting some imagined creative breakthrough. These true advertrocities—which have made my shocked lecture audiences howl with derision the world over—were seen by their makers as triumphs.

So there you have it. It is easy to be wrong when you're clois-
tered on the inside with like-minded, like-blinded people. It's easy
to be right when you are on the outside looking in.

This begs another question: well, if it's so damn easy, why hasn't
anyone done this before? And the answer to that one is: people have.
Over the years there have been a number of regular features criti-
cizing advertising on a variety of criteria. Many of them, of course,
came from outside advertising, from writers who used as a point of
departure the presumption that advertising is a sinister, malevolent
force bent on manipulating consumers' psyches and even overriding
their free will to pump sales of superfluous products the consumers
neither want nor need, the use of which will destroy the environment
while exploiting the downtrodden everywhere.

As if. As if advertising were an industry populated with omnipo-
tent Svengalis. As if anyone in the business were really that good.
While advertising has its excesses, it has historically proven to be
woefully poor at selling what people don't, of their own volition, care
to buy. The sad truth is, advertising has historically proven to be not
so hot at selling what people *do* of their own volition want to buy.
(Oh, sure, advertising works. Even somewhat inferior advertising
works. But—partly because its practitioners are so misguided about
how to ply their trade—most advertising only just barely accom-
plishes its benign mandate. This, too, is where I come in. But again
I digress.)

The second kind of ad criticism came from advertising publi-
cations themselves. Alas, signed critiques were historically puffy in
nature, written by ex–ad guys or working ad guys loath to be too
rough on their fellow travelers. Such systematic tossing of laurels,
naturally, is of dubious value. "Thumbs up" soon loses its meaning if
there is no possibility for thumbs down. As for *un*signed critiques,
they've often been more pointed, but their validity—not to mention
any potential conflict of interest—is obscured by their anonymity.

What the industry never had until the 1980s was an outsider, steeped in advertising history and business knowledge, uninfected by the Chicken Little orthodoxy of the eco-left, and unconnected to the industry itself to review individual ads, naming names, without fear or favor. Then came Barbara Lippert.

My colleague and competitor at *Adweek* magazine beat me to the gig by nearly three years. Her witty, provocative critiques—combining cultural anthropology, semiotics, and marketing principles to analyze ad content—quickly became her publication's most popular feature. When I was hired by *Ad Age* from *USA Today*, my job soon became to do approximately the same thing.

Key word: approximately.

While I also deal with advertising's place in the culture, among many other considerations, my focus has always been primarily on business. Does an ad succeed in furthering the client's strategy or doesn't it? And what about the strategy in the first place? Is it recognizable? Does it make sense? From the beginning in 1985, "Ad Review" raised these questions and tried to answer them, citing specific shortfalls and excesses, often enough in the bluntest terms.

Mind you, advertising is an industry long accustomed to meticulously crafting its own messages. It is an industry whose institutional self-reflection is confined to awarding one another gilded statuettes. It was not accustomed to taking sniper fire from trade magazines. Furthermore, adding insult to "Ad Review" injury, there was the star system. Back in 1986, *Ad Age's* then managing editor Valerie Mackie insisted that each review include a star rating, such as movie critics employ. I resisted, arguing that there are too many considerations—from acting to ethics to market share—to be synthesized into a single, meaningful value. Val was both unyielding and higher than me on the masthead, so, after a perfunctory display of dudgeon, I caved. The result is something akin to an advertising institution.

While I would love to take credit for astonishing vision and perspicacity, the fact is that the stars are what give "Ad Review" its clout. People in the industry who may dismiss my actual advice as brainless, or worse, nonetheless pay strict attention to the ratings, because in addition to being a shorthand, those stupid stars have become a sort of currency. Everyone knows what four "Ad Review" stars mean, and everyone knows what one star means, and in either case, on any given Monday, a lot of people are stargazing for the verdict. A glowing review, naturally, is used as a morale builder and client calmer downer and a new-business tool for the incumbent agency.

Oh, and I get a lot of kissy-assy little thank-you notes recognizing me for my good taste and canny judgment.

The real activity, however, is what follows an "Ad Review" trashing. Those are used as new-business tools, too—by sharks at other agencies who start faxing prospective clients at the first smell of blood. Clients also often contact agency managers with what diplomats call "a frank and candid exchange of ideas." This is sometimes followed by a frank and candid change of agencies. And sometimes individual ads or entire campaigns simply vanish. Sergio Zyman, when he was chief worldwide marketing executive for the Coca-Cola Co., killed a brand-new $200 million worldwide campaign by Monday afternoon after reading an "Ad Review" Monday morning delineating the campaign's many shortcomings.

Barbara's column, thoughtful as it is, has never had quite that effect.

This is not to suggest I fancy myself as some kind of power broker. While I am imbued with stunning insight and just oodles of charisma, a mover and shaker I do not pretend to be. Indeed, fulsome thank-you notes notwithstanding, and lacking any real research on the subject, my suspicion is that the typical reaction to a given negative column within a given agency is "Jeez, what a putz" and not much else. (Oddly, there are four or five agencies—agencies regarded as among the best in the world and that have fared extremely well over the years in "Ad Review"—that have given the matter more thought. Certain top executives from those shops, upon reading a negative appraisal in "Ad Review" and unable to see anything in the advertising that could possibly have warranted such abuse, conclude that I harbor some sinister "agenda." As if I lay awake at night scheming to destroy the total strangers at Fallon or whatever. It's like, gimme a break.)

Anyway, "Ad Review" nonetheless has evolved, as no such feature before it, into a force to be reckoned with. For those reasons, and remembering that I am never wrong, I can think of nobody better suited to promulgating the Ten Commandments of Advertising—which momentarily I shall descend the mount to share.

SORRY, NO CANNES DO

You should know, though, what finally prompted me after twenty years finally to do so, because—unlike a lot of advertising—it's relevant. What finally made me hear God's call was the Cannes International Advertising Film Festival.

Over those twenty years, Cannes has become the industry's preeminent awards venue. This is a consequence of cunning management combined with the ideal location, the cachet of the month-earlier Cannes Film Festival, and of course, the industry's inexhaustible supply of vanity. Eight thousand–some entries stream in each year, absolutely unfiltered—provided the attached checks don't bounce.

The results are eye-opening. To sit through the film screenings—one dreadful commercial after another—is to wonder by what delusions of competency these things got suggested, much less entered? By what standards of salesmanship did they get approved?

And by what twisted notion of decorum, never mind self-knowledge, do the all-in-blacks in the auditorium whistle and hiss at entries exactly as unwatchable as their own?

Hey, Dr. Advertising. Heal thyself.

No doubt there's a lot to be learned from the endless procession of clichés, cheesy productions, too-extravagant productions, preposterous dialogue, pointless vignettes, gratuitous sex, miscast celebrities, blaring rock-and-roll beds, ostentatious digital effects, vulgar jokes, obvious jokes, stolen jokes, mistimed jokes, unfunny jokes, irrelevant jokes, comical ghost entries, and seventy-three-second "directors' cuts." What's mainly to be learned is that good advertising is hard to do, that there's more to this game than a slick production and the desire to entertain, that the penalty for yielding to your worst impulses, among other things, is an audience full of your colleagues recognizing you for the fraud you are.

What the delegates seem to learn, however, is another lesson altogether—that resisting your impulses is unnecessary, because the bar is set very, very low. The catalog of shortcomings I've just described is not the experience of wandering into a screening room for, say, the entire unfiltered soft-drinks category. It's the experience of watching the judges' short list.

The pickings are so slim, because advertising industry is so gigantically misguided all around the world, that the Cannes juries are reduced each year to giving serious Lion consideration to ads that have gotten hissed out of the screening rooms by losers. Oh, certainly there are deserving winners, too. Elsewhere in these pages you'll find an accounting of genuine triumphs, masterful and even sublime executions of ingenious ideas. But what this festival reminds us of most is not how the greatest work soars, transcendently, into our hearts and imaginations. No, the sad lesson of this festival is that many practitioners of the business fail most of the time to do their jobs minimally well—and some of them get trophies for it.

This situation is not merely frustrating; it is outrageous. And Cannes, which should be part of the solution, is part of the problem.

Is it June, or is it May? Are you a screenwriter or a copywriter; a director or an art director? Who cares? Rush to that stage. Hoist that Lion. Bask in the lights. Win the applause of your colleagues. Get the big salary. Get the Porsche. Get a killer reel together. Get your own agency—not necessarily because you've moved much merchandise but because you are clever, clever, clever! And all the whistling wannabes want to be just like you. Only they are too clever, clever, clever by half, half, half. Now hit the Hotel Martinez bar, while, somewhere back in Ohio, the client sits at his desk sweating market share and thinking of firing your award-winning ass.

What's the difference? The guy's an ignoramus in wing-tipped cordovans. You had to sneak the damned spot past him. And there is a very leggy production-company rep striding your way. You, my friend, are a star.

And so the cycle goes.

Now, I certainly understand that this lament accompanies a certain, tired point of view—namely that advertising exists to help sell products and services and that any advertising that does not ultimately serve that end is unworthy of trophies, of adulation, of even consideration. I know there is a place somewhere—the Home for Retired Account Executives—filled with doddering old scolds muttering between gin games about self-indulgent young creatives who don't care to sell. ("Yo, Pops, did you like the latest lizards commer— "THAT'S NO COMMERCIAL! WHAT'S COMMERCIAL ABOUT THAT? ANACIN! 1961! NOW *THAT'S* A COMMERCIAL! *THAT'S....*")

My viewpoint is leavened somewhat by the understanding that agencies aren't necessarily stupid, that they themselves struggle with an inherent conflict of interest, because the kind of advertising that best serves the client doesn't necessarily win awards, and new business is won with a reception room full of trophies. It also presumes that clients bear equal responsibility for being bewitched by the trophy cases and for falling into the thrall of executive creative directors who do 93 percent of their selling in teak-paneled conference rooms.

And it also presumes that admonitions against entertainment value are both misguided and useless, because the very best advertising is itself extremely entertaining. It is itself enthralling, bewitching, and—often enough—very, very, very funny using exactly the same techniques as the stuff that embarrasses all of us to see every single day. Furthermore, as I'll later make abundantly clear, the days when the advertiser can artlessly bludgeon a consumer with a brand message are long gone. Not only is the industry still paying in consumer hostility for the days when such bludgeoning was commonplace, but the fragmented media world and the TV remote control offer instant escape from any commercial deemed insufficiently engaging.

Still, the fact remains: most advertising is unnecessarily terrible. And I am finished being sheepish about saying so, because—my word, I'd almost forgotten—I'm right. Thus it was in connection with Cannes that I had my sacred epiphany.

Because, periodically, I have to go there.

WORSHIPING FALSE IDOLS ON THE FRENCH RIVIERA

I was sitting on the airplane, heading for the Mecca of advertising excess, in a state of dread. About three thousand worshipers of Pointless Originality had already converged for their sun-drenched hajj— each of them, of course, dressed in black. It was festival time on the Côte de Noir, and I sat, en route, ruminating. What would happen there?

Duh. I knew damn well what would happen there. The usual would happen there. A handful of magnificent advertisements would be Lionized. A similar number of worthy advertisements would be dismissed. Thousands upon thousands of forgettable commercials would be screened to indifference. And one or two travesties would win gold instead of the scorn they deserved.

Cocktails would flow. Platinum cards would be flashed. Lavish meals would be expensed. Surreptitious glances would be stolen at young women with the best bodies money can build. Situational ethics would be invoked. Deals would be done. Some creatives would be inspired by what they saw. Many more would be reassured of their own singular genius. And the harbor would echo each morning with the slosh and rumble of the street-cleaning machines, accompanied by the shuffling footfalls of carousers retiring to the dawn.

I'd be one of them, adolescent immoderation being the contagion it is. Then, after seven days of high-priced hedonism, reality would resume. I would flee Gomorrah to do the same thing I've been doing for years. Unfortunately, so would everybody else. The Nice airport would overflow with the bleary-eyed, more exhausted by the experience than educated by it. Though they'd have witnessed, and applauded, two or three dozen dazzling solutions to daunting creative, strategic, or communications challenges, most would go back home having internalized all the wrong lessons. And the next year it all would happen again.

Why? Why? Why? There is simply no need for this to be.

To paraphrase Tolstoy, all good advertisements are alike; they all combine sound strategy with sound execution of a sound selling idea. But all bad advertisements are alike, too; they make the same few mistakes over and over and over. For a critic that truth represents an endless resource, a golden goose, a perpetual-motion machine. The ads break. I document these recurring flaws. The ads (usually) fail. Alas, whatever grim satisfaction I get out of being proven correct is

trumped by the utter futility of seeing the errors repeated, perenni-
ally, inexorably, by the same agencies and the same clients time and
again. And if the weekly water torture weren't enough, each June
there is Cannes. Full immersion.

No wonder I drink.

Well, something had to be done. The ensuing seven days played
out exactly as I'd known they would, and on the flight back I made
my compact with the Lord. I would serve as His angel on earth.

The result is the slender volume that follows, the advertising
Ten Commandments, guiding principles for all creative decisions all
the time. Don't expect an inclusive list of how to do strong advertising; that would be quixotic and presumptuous even for me. Anyway,
God didn't say "Thou shalt consider conflict resolution." He said,
"Thou shalt not kill." Most of what you'll find in this book, accord-
ingly, is guidance on what *not* to do—as well as what not to believe,
not to think, and not to delude yourself about. The emphasis is on
television commercials, because that is the medium I have most concerned myself with. The underlying principles, however, apply across
the board, from TV to print to Internet to bas-relief molded in the
sea-coastal sand.

Much of what you'll find here I have written about before; some
is adapted (i.e., lifted wholesale) from critical disquisition in *Ad Age*
and elsewhere—so apologies to anyone in my enormous worldwide
cult of followers who, encountering certain passages, feel an eerie
sensation of déjà vu. That ends my list of apologies, however. Yes,
much of what you will find here is anathema to many if not most of
the industry's current practitioners, but it is not anathema rendered
frivolously. It is the distillation of many years of thought about advertising, and if it creates a little irritation now, I expect it will also save
a lot of people a lot of embarrassment in the south of France. In fact,
in writing this, that's my only goal.

Wait. Did I say *"will* save a lot of people a lot of embarrassment"? Make that *could.* Or *should.* As Moses discovered the hard way, the prophet business is a bitch. I'd be naive to imagine that all the tribes of advertising will read these instructions and suddenly change their idolatrous ways. In fact I'd be naive to imagine appearing at the next Cannes festival and *not* finding the all-in-blacks worshiping a golden Lion. But if that happens, from this day forward, nobody can blame me. I've put in my forty days and forty nights and then some. At this point all I can do is pray.

Perhaps you are familiar with the greatest commercial ever made, by Chiat/Day and director Ridley Scott, introducing the Apple Macintosh computer. The scenario was a futuristic, Orwellian nightmare. The tag line was, "So 1984 [the year] won't have to be like *1984* [the novel]." Well, fair enough. Think of this book as why, at long last, thanks to my sainted efforts, if anybody cares to heed the wisdom of the ages, Cannes won't have to be like Cannes.

Thank God.

DISCLAIMER

This book is filled with examples of advertising blunders so egregious you will go lightheaded. Due to bad luck and nothing else, certain agencies will have the privilege of seeing several of their advertrocities paraded for public view. Do not jump to any conclusions. Saatchi & Saatchi, to cite one of the unfortunate, has created tens of thousands of ads in its corporate history and has had more than its share of triumphs for British Air, the Tory party, and many other clients. The same goes for Leo Burnett, Hal Riney & Partners, Fallon, BBDO, and any other organization that takes it disproportionately on the chin in this manifesto. Any single agency's over- or underrepresentation here reveals absolutely nothing but the luck of the draw.

RULES ARE MADE TO BE OBSERVED

So, you know, I was reading *Swann's Way*, by Marcel Proust . . . just reading a little Proust one day . . . and while reading Proust, I happened upon a line that intrigued me. (Actually, I happened upon it quite often, because I've started that book at least seven times and never gotten past page 175, because this guy was positively soporific. Having a little insomnia at bedtime? May I suggest a little Proust? You'll be out like Rosie O'Donnell within six pages.)

But it so happened that Proust, the nineteenth-century French novelist/sleep aid, made a striking observation. It was about poets, "whom the tyranny of rhyme forces into the discovery of their finest lines."

His point was that the rigid poetic form focuses a writer's thinking. The need to contrive a rhyme forces the poet to measure every subtle shade of meaning and to be judicious with every syllable. While a given stanza offers a vast lexicon of options for expressing a thought, it is not nearly the daunting, infinite number of possibilities in the realm of unrhymed blank verse or—more daunting still—

unrhymed, metrically unregulated free verse. Bearing no responsibility for meter and rhyme, the author of free verse is free to be sloppy, flabby, imprecise. The author of rhyme must find just the right vivid solution—a solution that, minus the tyrant, might never have otherwise suggested itself.

Rhyme, of course, in incapable hands, can lead to hackneyed couplets like the worst-laid plans. But in the hands of an artist, it can be the stuff of magic.

> *The curfew tolls the knell of parting day,*
> *The lowing herd wind slowly o'er the lea,*
> *The plowman homeward plods his weary way,*
> *And leaves the world to darkness and to me.*

That's the first stanza of Thomas Gray's "Elegy Written in a Country Churchyard," and I dare say you can feel the exhaustion of the day's end, which is here a metaphor for life's end. The tyrant, rhyme, here is proved to be an enlightened despot indeed. (Oh, by the way, "lea," pronounced *lee*, is a pasture. Read it again if you have to.)

THE TYRANNY OF FREEDOM AND VICE VERSA

Loosening by tightening; Proust wasn't the only French thinker to observe this paradox. The sixteenth-century philosopher Michel de Montaigne also considered the liberating beauty of form. (And, as God is my witness, this one didn't come from Bartlett's *Familiar Quotations* either. I ran across this one reading the collected musings of Montaigne himself. I won't explain to you how this came to pass. I'll simply leave you to be quietly awed.) Anyway, Montaigne noted that the sweet sound of the trumpet results from the physics of constriction: ". . . as the voice, forced through the narrow passage of a trumpet, comes out more forcible and shrill; so, methinks, a sentence pressed within the harmony of verse, darts out more briskly upon the understanding, and strikes my ear and apprehension with a smarter and more pleasing effect." He and Proust were making identical points: what superficially may look confining is, in fact, the path to liberty. (For the moment we shall ignore that when another philosopher, Nietzsche, ruminated on the ruminations of yet another philosopher, Kant, on the very same subject, the concept of freedom by repression was seized by Hitler as a rationalization for totalitarianism. *Arbeit macht frei*, my ass.) Here's a little Shakespeare:

> *When, in disgrace with fortune and men's eyes,*
> *I all alone beweep my outcast state*
> *And trouble deaf heaven with my bootless cries*
> *And look upon myself and curse my fate,*
> *Wishing me like to one more rich in hope,*
> *Featur'd like him, like him with friends possess'd,*
> *Desiring this man's art and that man's scope,*
> *With what I most enjoy contented least;*
> *Yet in these thoughts myself almost despising,*
> *Haply I think on thee, and then my state,*
> *Like to the lark at break of day arising*
> *From sullen earth, sings hymns at heaven's gate;*
> *For thy sweet love remember'd such wealth brings*
> *That then I scorn to change my state with kings.*

Nice work. It is wrought in fourteen lines of iambic pentameter—three quatrains followed by a couplet in the rhyming scheme ab, ab, cd, cd, ef, ef, gg. He wrote 154 just like it. That was number 29. Here's number 6:

Then let not winter's ragged hand deface
In thee thy summer, ere thou be distill'd:
Make sweet some vial; treasure thou some place
With beauty's treasure, ere it be self-kill'd.
That use is not forbidden usury,
Which happies those that pay the willing loan;
That's for thyself to breed another thee,
Or ten times happier, be it ten for one;
Ten times thyself were happier than thou art,
If ten of thine ten times refigured thee:
Then what could death do, if thou shouldst depart,
Leaving thee living in posterity?
Be not self-will'd, for thou art much too fair
To be death's conquest and make worms thine heir.

It's hard to say which sonnet is more magnificent, but I'm just curious. Did you happen to notice anything, apart from the rigid constraints of the form, remotely similar in the two works? Similar language? Similar themes? Similar imagery? Actually, I can answer that question: no, you didn't, because the two sonnets, apart from fourteen lines of iambic pentameter, have nothing whatsoever in common. The first is about how even the biggest loser feeling sorry for himself is uplifted by the life jacket of love. The second is a recipe for immortality: have children, nuisance though they may be. So, once again, the Bard of Avon didn't seem too hamstrung by form, did he?

For crying out loud, you needn't turn to Shakespeare or Proust to understand this lesson. Just talk to any child psychologist. Children need rules. The lack of boundaries does not liberate; it enslaves, trapping the frightened child in an anxiety-provoking world of consequences he cannot control. Discipline, a firm establishment of boundaries, relieves kids from the terror of uncertainty. If you want an insecure child, give in to his every tantrum and whim. If you want a happy, well-adjusted kid, learn to say no and mean it. Needless to add, this is equally true of adults. "Good fences," Robert Frost famously observed, "make good neighbors." They also make good art directors.

So why in advertising—when it is well established among artists that there is nothing so intimidating as a blank piece of paper—this preposterous cult of rule breaking? Rule breaking, in fact, if we are to take seriously all the industry's widespread and ostentatious claims of iconoclasm, has itself become the rule. Every corner of advertising, in every corner of the world, is populated with people who imagine themselves to be courageous anarchists. Bob Schmetterer, chairman of Messner, Vetere, Schmetterer, Berger, McNamee/Euro RSCG traveled to Cannes to speechify on "Breaking the Rules." The introduction to the TBWA website proclaims: "Change the Rules." Korey Kay & Partners, the New York agency, asks prospective clients to declare *in writing* whether they'd be willing to break the rules. Even DDB chairman Keith Reinhard, the soft-spoken and conscientious midwesterner, claimed, in a speech before the American Association of Advertising Agencies, to be a "rule breaker."

All that mischievousness! But wait, there's more! Because the same "philosophy" has spread, like spitting sunflower seeds in the dugout, from the big leagues to the minors.

On its website, the Virtual Farm agency in Pennsylvania has promised prospects great ideas that break the rules. GreenDOT Advertising has used its site to explain it's wise to break the rules, but only if you know what you're doing. (GreenDOT claimed to possess such rarefied knowledge. They *all* claim to possess such rarefied knowledge.) Fellers & Co., a Texas marketing and advertising group, brags that its creatives "Break the Rules." BananaDog Communications, the Australian web designer, lists as its corporate philosophy, "Our goals and visions are to break the rules." Lines Advertising &

Design says that "The Only rule to follow in developing an idea is not to have any rules." Web banner creator Dave Nixon lists ten rules for banner design in descending order, culminating in Rule No. 1: "Break the rules." Corinthian Media, the media-buying company, admonishes prospective customers, "Don't be afraid to break the rules." Self-described marketing guru Dan Kennedy's book is titled *How to Succeed in Business by Breaking All the Rules*. And how-to instructor Robert W. Bly explains, "The top copywriters succeed because they know when to break the rules."

And lest you imagine that this is just a domestic phenomenon, please note the theme for the Asian Federation of Advertising Associations' AdAsia 2003: "Break the Rules."

Here's some not Proust:

> *I, I wanna be bad*
> *You make bad feel so good*
> *I'm losing all my cool*
> *I'm about to break the rules*
> *I, I wanna be bad*
> *I wanna be bad with ya, baby*
> *I, I, I, I, I wanna be bad, baby*

From "I Wanna Be Bad." Copyright 2000 by Willa Ford.

Yessiree, baby, if you wanna be bad, set out boldly to break the rules. Then you can hardly fail. For instance, several of the agencies I just mentioned are long since out of business. And, of course, who can forget Burger King's 1989–90 ad slogan "Sometimes You've Gotta Break the Rules"? The spectacular crashing, burning failure of that campaign, leaving the client in flame-broiled cinders, is testament to the abject vacuity of the proposition. Yet, as we have seen, every creative director and his brother speaks of smashing barriers, violating taboos, pushing the envelope. Why? Who says the envelope needs to be pushed? In most cases the writer, the client, and the consumer would be far better served if the envelope were simply stuffed, stamped, and sent on its way. The path to market-share hell is paved with brands that actually had relevant, differentiating news to deliver—the kind of brand-benefit news most marketers would sell their mothers' kidneys to be able to exploit—only to indulge in some eccentric notion of inspired misfeasance.

THIS JUST IN: TRANSPORTATION TRANSPORTS

One vivid example was the introduction, by the Mullen agency of Wenham, Massachusetts, in 1997, of General Motors Certified Used Vehicles. The cover letter that accompanied the reel to the "Ad Review" Viewing Laboratory began as follows: "Only a few times in the past 100 years has General Motors introduced a new brand. Recently, the GM Certified Used Vehicles brand was launched and now takes its place alongside Saturn, Chevrolet, Pontiac, Oldsmobile and Cadillac." So evidently this was a momentous occasion, although the agency left a couple of things out:

1. The entire Buick Motor Division
2. Any sense whatsoever, in the actual advertising campaign, about what this new brand was supposed to be

By 1997 other manufacturers had long since established certified-used-vehicle programs. As a late entry, the agency determined, GM had to do something different, daring, unexpected. So, in introducing certified used vehicles, General Motors ignored the "certified" and the "used" parts of the advertised brand and paid homage, eventually, at the end of sixty-second commercials, to . . . *the con-*

venience of vehicles. Turned out, and I hope you're sitting down, that cars and vans are very good at transporting people.

One spot featured a montage of children playing various sports. It started with three hockey players emerging from a garage, then a chubby little golfer, then a yawning girl swimmer. The audio track was some coach giving encouragement: "You guys are the champions, you know that? All right, let me see those game faces. That's it." Then, in reverse type, the word *love* appeared on the screen, and a little girl said, "We need love." Then the coach exhorted his team: "We're out here to play baseball, right?" "Right!" the kids shouted back. Then the word *encouragement* flashed up, and a girl reiterated, "We need encouragement." The next two images showed one pair of kids dressed up for a dance, another pair for a Halloween party. Then a kid in front of a fighter plane. The next buzzword: *inspiration.* "We need inspiration."

At that stage the ad seemed like your basic, aspirational Nike commercial. But then came a wonderfully charming shot of a kid dressed in a dog costume fashioned entirely out of empty twelve-ounce cans. Then a little girl angrily walking down the sidewalk, having just been in a fight. (Dad: "She didn't start it." Mom: "It doesn't really matter who started it.") This led to the next human quality kids require adults to furnish: "We need understanding." Then, finally, after shots of a boy violinist and a sullen little girl in a leotard, came the ultimate thing kids need:

Rides.

And, sure enough, the ad documented hockey players and the dancer and the tin-can dog waiting around for the grown-ups to pick them up. In a minivan. (Which make you couldn't tell, because it was a bird's-eye view.) Then, finally, the voice-over jumped in to tell you the point—or, at least, the sponsor—of all this moral and practical instruction: "Introducing used vehicles. Reconditioned, warrantied, and ready for life. GM Certified."

Get it? Kids need understanding *and* chauffeur service. In the second spot, some equally trenchant news: salesmen need cars. And so, presumably, we were to be moved by how this new GM brand understands our lives.

Terrific. So what? What good could that understanding possibly do us? While Mullen's slices of life were indeed precious, we didn't need Certified Used Vehicles to lecture us on loving and encouraging kids. We have Hillary Clinton for that. As for the revelation that automobiles are useful, well . . . duh. The problem wasn't that the ads belabored the obvious. It was that the ads belabored the *wrong* obvious. Never mind the benefits of love and automobiles. Where are the stores? How are the prices? What kind of warranty?

Oh, and, by any chance, do they sell used Buicks? So, yes, the campaign was unexpected, all right. And, of course, also unsuccessful. GM and Mullen soon parted ways. In marriage and the agency business, so often, rule breaking results in relationship breaking.

WILL REFRACT FOR FOOD

Maybe you look at that example and say, "*That's* breaking the rules? Calvin Klein does kiddie porn commercials, and *a used-car montage* is subversive?" But I started with that one on purpose, because in attempting to forge some sort of emotional bond with the viewer, it breaks the most fundamental advertising rule of all: if you have news to deliver, deliver it. Consumers are actually eager to have information. It is one of the few things they actually value about advertising, so to squander that opportunity in favor of getting sentimental over secondhand Luminas is absolutely unforgivable.

Alas, while that example is certainly a bit infuriating, it's also basic and unremarkable. My goal here isn't to leave you a bit infuriated. My goal is to enumerate transgressions so extravagant and insane that you actually bleed through the ears.

So let's take a moment to revisit the extraordinary, rule-breaking, barrier-smashing, envelope-pushing 1994 For Eyes campaign, from the Beber/Silverstein agency in Miami. This whole-grain eyewear chain, founded by ex-hippie opticians (!), had amassed a fortune selling discount eyeglasses. Its peace-and-love values remained intact, however, and its corporate principles regarded the use of advertising merely to sell goods and services to be just, like, *sooooo* old paradigm. Therefore, in a series of fifteen-second spots the advertiser contrived to combine a commercial with a message of social responsibility. The most astonishing of these let the camera linger on homeless men living like society's refuse in a city park. "If you've grown used to this, you need glasses," the public-spirited portion of the ad observed, its figurative finger wagging in the face of the viewer.

Then, the second portion of the message: "Two pairs for $79."

Well, it broke the rules, all right, as seldom before in the history of commerce had a marketer so daringly juxtaposed unspeakable human tragedy, on the one hand, with attractive discount pricing, on the other. The campaign was on for less than a week when it was pulled, in response to viewer outrage. The agency was soon fired for talking the client into what, for my money, is the single worst TV commercial ever made.

Of course, it *wasn't* my money, was it? It was the client's money. It's always the client's money. How easy it is to break the rules when somebody else is footing the bill.

In subsequent chapters I'll describe many such mind-boggling blunders in sickening detail, along with the associated costs to those clients gulled into signing off on them. For the moment, though, let's revisit a car campaign that famously broke the rules in August of 1989, quickly found itself water-cooler conversation from coast to coast, vaulting into the nation's consciousness as few product introductions ever do, and has been paying the price ever since.

You remember it, too. It was the unveiling of the long-awaited Japanese luxury-car line Infiniti, a debut so enamored of its Taoist imagery that it engendered an inscrutable Eastern conundrum: what is the point of no cars driving? Nine commercials from Hill, Holliday, Connors, Cosmopulos featured beautiful scenes of nature's serenity and no automobile whatsoever. Not a one.

Trees in the distance, rustling in the breeze.

That was the image—the only image—in the spot called "Distant Leaves." Just a long shot of windblown trees, with a voice-over narration in a calm, putatively conversational tone, not much more than a whisper: "The car is connected to an engine, a suspension system. The car fits in the road, which fits in a landscape. And when all of this—the will of the driver, the ability of the car, the feel of the road—when all of that is one thing, together, then you get a sense, a true idea of luxury. Infiniti."

Other spots had names like "Flock of Geese" and "Delicate Branches" and "Misty Tree"—each with the same spare style, the same fixation with some bit of Washington state naturalism and the same nonmention of antilock brakes or McPherson struts. In "Summer Storm," which showed distant lightning over a lake at dusk, the narrator said, trying his level best to sound unnarratorlike: "You know, it's not just a car, it's an expression of the culture, an aesthetic that is connected somehow to nature, a way of saying 'This is what we can do if we work at the highest level of our potential.' That's the level of the commitment behind a new line of luxury cars from Japan. Infiniti."

Swell, but does it have power windows?

The answer, of course, was the basis for the whole campaign: *certainly* there were power windows. Certainly the entire line of new

Infinitis had amazing engines, marvelous suspensions, and every appointment you could think of—just like Acura did and rival new-entry Lexus did and, come to think of it, General Motors did. Nissan Motor Corp., which owns Infiniti, and the agency well understood that quality and comfort were hardly distinguishing qualities. By 1989 the luxury-car marketplace was glutted and getting glutteder. To prosper under those circumstances, to enjoy the fat margins of the luxury segment, to win the hearts and minds of consumers with $40,000+ to spend to be backed up on the freeway, they believed that simply having a great car would not do.

So they decided to take the focus off the car.

It was a strategy based on novelty (How could that not get attention?) and psychographics, aiming at the large, barely tapped market of affluent young people who regard luxury cars as vulgar emblems. They know a Jaguar is a beautiful automobile, but they also know owning one is the automotive equivalent of neck jewelry. They are inconspicuous consumers, and the car-free launch of Infiniti was an attempt to seize their imaginations not with slick product shots but with ideas. Or, at least, with the illusion of ideas. The copy was mainly a lot of pseudospiritual drivel, and the studiously conversational narrative more pompous than authentic.

"A new vision, more idealistic," the narrator intoned in a spot called "Rain with Branches." "The time has come, the walrus said. The time has come. Infiniti."

Oy vey. In search of the paradoxically inconspicuous consumer: an exercise in paradoxically pretentious understatement. But if part of the goal was to generate attention, that it did. Oh, did it ever. Within weeks, Infiniti—the car company too embarrassed to display its cars—was a national laughingstock. Jay Leno, in his "Tonight Show" monologue, reported that Infiniti showrooms were empty, but "I understand that the sale of rocks and trees is up 300 percent."

Truthfully, the campaign wasn't awful. In its conception, at least as a teaser, it made sense. But the advertiser and the agency became so seduced by the uproar the ads were generating that they—like so many misguided souls—mistook awareness for affection. Having gotten the American public even more curious about the look of the new cars, they, for the second phase of the campaign, pushed all their chips onto the same number. That's right: they barely showed the car in those spots either. Lexus, meanwhile, had its handsome models in America's face constantly, with copy aimed not at those who desire luxury to fulfill some sort of Zen concept of automotive perfection but at those who wish to impress the living crap out of their neighbors.

At the end of the first year, Lexus sold more than twice as many cars as Infiniti, an advantage that has only grown larger. In 2001, Lexus's U.S. market share for cars and light trucks was 1.3 percent. Infiniti's was .4 percent—leaving one to wonder why the conventional wisdom puts such a premium on being unconventional.

THE "1984" PARADOX

I keep asking why that's so, but, come on, I know why. One reason is that advertising creatives, as a class, seem to be caught up in their own Myth of the Cutting Edge, that they are somehow dangerous agents provocateurs, daring young men doing high-wire work without a net, artists who substantially define themselves by redefining the status quo. As we shall see in Chapter 7 ("Are You Doomed? Take This Simple Quiz!"), I don't think that is healthy, productive thinking, but we shall get to this later. The second reason is the "1984" Paradox.

The spot called "1984"—as noted in the introduction to this extraordinary literary event—was probably the greatest commercial in the history of advertising. Created by Chiat/Day and directed by the legendary Ridley Scott, it depicted a futuristic Orwellian nightmare in which a tyrannical Big Brother ranted, via telescreen, to an auditorium full of devolved, slack-jawed drones.

But as they sit there—glassy-eyed and monochromatic—down the aisle runs a young woman, slim and strong and supple. She is wielding a track-and-field hammer, which she whips round and round until she finally unleashes it toward the huge telescreen. Big Brother's image disappears in the shattering explosion. The slaves are freed. Then the voice-over: "Introducing the Apple Macintosh. So 1984 won't have to be like *1984*."

Get it? Big Brother is IBM, the looming, information-dominating tyrant, and Macintosh is the fearless liberator—a tool and (more important) a symbol of independence for the heroic iconoclast. Nowadays, needless to say, that sounds ridiculous, because in no way, shape, or form is IBM the omniscient, omnivorous Big Brother. Obviously, Microsoft is Big Brother. But back in 1984 the landscape was a little different, and this commercial was an emotion-laden masterpiece.

It was also—by any ordinary measure of linear, logical, left-brained, informative communication—one of the most irrational acts in advertising history. Think about it. The personal-computing world at that time was a DOS world. Not a Windows-overlaying-DOS world. Just plain ugly, unadorned, C-prompt-intensive DOS. So here comes this revolutionary, user-friendly new technology that introduces the idea of icons and a handheld mouse with which to navigate around applications. And the commercial—the Super Bowl commercial introducing this extraordinary new technology to the world—*doesn't include so much as a product shot.*

How's that for pushing the envelope?

It was an astonishing gamble that has paid off in incalculable ways. For instance, forgetting for a moment the commercial's vaunted place in history, at this writing eighteen years later, this defiant, psychographic appeal is still the very core of all Apple marketing, all the time. "Think Different" and "1984" are fundamentally identical.

So there you have it. The greatest commercial of all time—perhaps the greatest single advertisement of all time—broke every rule imaginable. Indeed, much of the greatest advertising breaks every rule imaginable; its very genius resides in the unexpected path it takes to make an impact on the consumer. I'm thinking, for instance, of Volkswagen's "Lemon," Clairol's "Does she . . . or doesn't she?" and Nike's "Just Do It."

The problem is, those are three examples. Each year at least three hundred thousand ads are produced—and maybe it's three million—and a shocking percentage of them violate the rules, too, under the pitiful, misguided belief that such is the road to Greatness. But that is not the road to Greatness. It is the road to Extreme Suckiness. If you've been to Cannes, and sat in the screening rooms as these would-be tours de force roll by one after another, you understand how pervasive is this cult of lawlessness and how consequently ubiquitous is the suckitude. A visit to the International Advertising Film Festival, or most any other awards competition, is a voyage to Suckville.

The "1984" paradox raises big questions for agencies as well. Do you cultivate an atmosphere of anarchy and derring-do, encouraging your employees to make all the wrong choices in a futile search for the breakthrough idea? Or do you enforce rational protocols for communication that are unlikely to result in the next "1984" but will improve the overall agency output by orders of magnitude?

Most agencies seem to have opted for the former. In my soon-to-be-announced agency, Garfield & God, things will be done a lot differently—because, as it turns out, discipline and genius are by no means mutually exclusive. In fact, let's try a little exercise here; let's scan the twenty-five greatest advertising campaigns, as declared a few years back by *Advertising Age*, and vet them for rule breaking. Apple, Volkswagen, Nike, Clairol, Avis ("We're number two. We try harder.") clearly took approaches revolutionary in their categories and counterintuitive according to all that advertising had writ holy. And, just to show you I'm not stacking the deck, I'll even throw in the Burma-Shave's road signs in verse, although they were really just a small-scale copycat idea that mushroomed into a phenomenon (turned out the tyrant, rhyme, didn't bat 1.000): WITHIN THIS VALE/OF TOIL AND SIN/YOUR HEAD GROWS BALD/BUT NOT YOUR CHIN/BURMA-SHAVE. The other nineteen campaigns—the other *nineteen*—broke not a single thing but sales records.

Coca-Cola ("The pause that refreshes"); Miller Lite ("Tastes great, less filling"); Federal Express ("Absolutely, positively overnight"); Alka-Seltzer; Pepsi-Cola ("Pepsi-Cola hits the spot"); DeBeers ("A diamond is forever"); Maxwell House ("Good to the last drop"); Ivory Soap ("99$^{44}/_{100}$% pure"); American Express ("Do you know me?"); Anacin ("Fast, fast relief"); Burger King ("Have it your way"); *Rolling Stone* ("Perception vs. reality"); and Campbell's Soup ("Mmm, mmm good") focused on intrinsic product benefits.

Marlboro (the Marlboro cowboy); McDonald's ("You deserve a break today"); the U.S. Army ("Be all that you can be"); and Pepsi ("the Pepsi Generation") reflected back on the aspirations of the target audience. Chanel ("Share the fantasy"), Absolut vodka (the bottle-shape campaign), and Hathaway ("the man in the Hathaway shirt") cultivated a sophisticated image.

Every one of those campaigns turned not on insurrection but on insight, understanding the brand and the consumer and forging a message to forge a bond between the two. Just for the record—and you'll just have to take my word for this, because I'll be damned if I'm going to list the whole lot of them—79 of *Ad Age*'s top 100 campaigns are as noncounterintuitive as can be. The people who created them understood that rules are made to be observed. Or, as my pal

Montaigne put it in 1575: "We should not easily change a law received." To wit:

USA Today, September 28, 1989: Burger King's new ad slogan is more than a sales pitch. It's a battle cry.

"Sometimes You've Gotta Break The Rules" is a daring tack for the nation's No. 2 restaurant chain, but desperate times call for daring moves. Since 1986, Burger King has seen its share of the hamburger market chipped away to 16.8% from 17.7% by a series of almost laughingly inept ad campaigns. During that time, No. 1 McDonald's has climbed from an estimated 30% to 35%. And what remaining company spirit "Herb the Nerd" and other lame ads didn't destroy, internal strife snuffed out. Restaurant quality and cleanliness began to slip—the early signs of death in the fast-food business.

As 800 employees digested the new campaign at a special screening here Wednesday, the company's marketing chief put the magnitude of the challenge in perspective. "We're trying to start a whole new company here, folks," said Gary L. Langstaff. "Don't look back."

Advertising Age, January 29, 1990: Three and a half months into a new marketing program, Burger King franchisees are grumbling about the umbrella ad theme. . . .

"The ['Sometimes you just gotta break the rules'] theme is completely ineffective," said Gary Robison, a Denver-area operator. "You've got to explain it to most people." Denver franchisee Nick Kraft said, "It's hard to understand, and the message is confusing." The director of operations for three West Coast franchises said the theme is causing problems more serious than confusion.

"What does 'Break the rules' mean?" asked this operator, who requested anonymity. "Some customers believe they can get anything they want, and for free." He said one customer who was told he couldn't get six packets of barbecue sauce for his 69¢ bag of fries responded, "Hey, you advertise that you gotta break rules."

Associated Press, February 27, 1991: Burger King's top marketing executive resigned Wednesday even as the nation's second-biggest hamburger chain is considering scrapping the "Sometimes you've gotta break the rules" advertising theme he developed.

Advertising Age, **April 22, 1991:** Burger King last week introduced its new theme, "Your way. Right away," backed by its old "Have it your way" jingle, in a new 30-second network TV spot for its BK Broiler. It ended the controversial 19-month tenure of "Sometimes you've gotta break the rules."

CHAPTER 2

ORIGINAL SIN

Perhaps you are wondering, "Bob, can you relate any amusing anecdotes about obscure, nineteenth-century German musicians, which anecdote will, in several material ways, be relevant to the fascinating subject of this thought-provoking chapter?"

Excellent question. Darn tootin', I can.

Let us for a moment consider Hans Guido von Bülow, the composer of such romantic piano works as *Iphigenie in Aulis Rêverie Fantastique* and *Tarantella Valse Caractéristique*. While his compositions are well regarded, von Bülow was most famous for two things:

1. Wielding a mighty baton. He was among the first "virtuoso" conductors, flamboyantly adding his imprimatur to the works he conducted. His interpretations of Richard Wagner are deemed especially sensitive.
2. Not wielding a mighty baton. His wife, Cosima, ditched him for Wagner.

Yet even as one of Europe's most prominent cuckolds, von Bülow was a powerful, influential man whose musical blessing was sought after by many a young composer. One day, as the story goes, the conductor agreed to listen to the composition of an ambitious youngster whose name is lost to history. Von Bülow was expecting not much at all and was shocked to witness the young man take a seat at the piano and unfurl one magnificent musical passage after another. He was shocked mainly because every single one of the melodic elements had been lifted wholesale from other composers of the day. Nonetheless, when the student finished playing, he looked expectantly at von Bülow and asked, "Maestro, how do you like it?"

Von Bülow answered positively. "I have always liked it," he said.

I CAN'T BELIEVE IT'S NOT LIBEL!

I invoke the von Bülow anecdote for three reasons. First, the question of originality is so often at the heart of advertising decisions, and within the industry contempt for those who display lack of originality—or, worse yet, a little bit of larceny—is very nearly universal.

The second reason is that, as you may have noted, the eager, musical plagiarist in question is not only anonymous but dead for approximately one hundred years—unlike certain currently living advertising professionals with hard-earned reputations and access to quality legal counsel. Therefore please note: in the examples that lace this chapter, nobody is making any accusations. This is not investigative advertising journalism. Nobody's integrity is being called into question. And if it seems that way, it shouldn't. Obviously—when it comes, for example, to two commercials that are virtually identical— nobody has necessarily copycatted anything. Coincidences happen all the time. *It's probably just a big misunderstanding.*

Still, if the subject is originality, we must begin with the presumption that this is a value that should be treasured above all, because in its absence creativity is in jeopardy, integrity is at stake, and advertising is ill-served. Eh?

- In 1986, a campaign for Belgium's Douwe Egberts coffee (Grey, Europe, Brussels) appeared in Cannes, tracking the rugged odyssey of a mythical coffee buyer to Colombia and back. In 1997, a Chiat/Day campaign for Nissan Pathfinder was a six-part adventure about a fictional couple on a little ride in the country. Oh, the country was in South America. The mapping of the journey, tracing the route onscreen, was done exactly as it had been done in the coffee series.
- A 1991 Chiat/Day commercial for NutraSweet titled "Blah, Blah, Blah"—filled with copy that went "Blah, blah, blah"— was virtually identical to a 1989 Ally & Gargano ad for Dunkin' Donuts called "Blah, Blah, Blah," which was filled with copy that went "Blah, blah, blah."
- A 2000 spot from DDB, Amsterdam, for Central Beheer insurance, was about a jealous cement-truck operator dumping his mixer's contents into the convertible of a man he incorrectly assumed to be courting his wife. This was somewhat similar to a 1998 commercial from Campbell Mithun Esty, Minneapolis, for K Mart's Route 66 jeans, in which a jealous cement-truck operator dumped his mixer's contents into the convertible of a man he incorrectly assumed to be courting his wife.
- A dreadful 1993 Slovenian commercial for KM meats by the Ljubljana agency Formitas appeared at Cannes. It was about a court food taster who feigned poisoning to frighten the king and his court from the table, whereupon he feasted on the banquet. Four years later, on the Super Bowl, the National

Pork Producers Council ran an identical vignette, courtesy of Bozell, Chicago. It sucked, too.

➤ Finally, there was the 1989 Cannes Grand Prix for the Spanish national television network, about a dog going to ridiculous, escalating, special-effects-assisted extremes to get his master's attention. Two years later, US West came out with a spot about a dog going to ridiculous, escalating, special-effects-assisted extremes to get *his* master's attention.

Those are but a few of many examples of . . . uh . . . like I said . . . *big misunderstandings*. And I think there is a tendency for most creative people to look at such misunderstandings and feel contempt, or at least pity, for those involved. If you, as I do, respect and value the raw imagination behind our greatest advertising, at a minimum you have to squirm in your chair to see work trading on other people's ideas. The US West spot, for instance, was sent to me by a PR woman from the Martin Agency in Richmond, Virginia. Two days later, as PR people are wont to do, she followed up with a phone call.

"Did the package arrive?" she asked.

There was no real need to respond. She knew the package had arrived. Packages always arrive. What she really wanted to know was, did I open the package, did I look at the tape, and did I like it?

"Yes," I said. "It arrived."

"Did you like it?" she asked.

"I have always liked it," I replied.

The PR woman, apparently a woeful ignoramus in the area of nineteenth-century German musical romanticism, didn't pick up the allusion—just as not one-tenth of 1 percent of the viewers of the US West spot detected it as the big misunderstanding it clearly was. Which raises the question: was it, then, an outrageous misunderstanding? If an idea is stolen in the forest, and nobody is around to notice it, does it make a difference?

That's not a rhetorical question. I can answer it. The answer is no. As long as there is no intersection of audiences, there is absolutely no reason why an idea that worked—or even failed—in Spain can't be expropriated and imported here.

I mean, for the most part, God was probably right. You shouldn't kill, except under the most dire circumstances, such as someone in the supermarket express aisle with sixteen items and a checkbook. You should not worship false idols, not even Springsteen. And you should certainly honor your father and mother, because without them you would have none of the neuroses that make you so special. But with this "Thou shalt not steal" thing . . . well, uh, dear Lord, just do me a little favor. Please check out a 1996 spot from Bartle Bogle Hegarty, London, for Faberge's Lynx cologne and then define *steal*. Because seldom have sixty seconds of TV advertising owed a debt to so many sources.

The scene was a chichi cocktail party, full of overwrought "beautiful people" and lots of wide-angle close-ups to accentuate the grotesquerie. The scene had elements of Fellini and equal parts *Midnight Cowboy*, *The Graduate*, and *Stardust Memories*.

The hero was a single young guy, awkward and out of his element but trying unsuccessfully to play it cool. Early on he wolfed down an hors d'oeuvre but found it inedible. So he spit it out, à la Tom Hanks in *Big*. Next we saw him as a clumsy Woody Allen type, trying to impress a gorgeous woman by leaning casually against a mannequin he thought would support his weight. It didn't. Over he went—springing back up ridiculously, but familiarly, just as Peter Sellers's Inspector Clouseau used to do.

Humiliated, he retreated to a powder room to regain his composure and discovered a bottle of Lynx cologne. Spraying it all over himself, he was suddenly transformed into a Jim Carrey–esque weirdo hyperstud, complete with the hairdo. All very cute—even if we'd seen it all before. Indeed the familiarity of the gags had nothing on the familiarity of the strategy. The self-mocking style and hyper-bolic premise of the ad were themselves a direct lift from sixties-era American men's cologne Hai Karate. The same ironic claim of instant irresistibility, the same sense of whimsy, the same everything.

Steal? This ad wantonly looted from every address in Media-ville. With no harm to anybody, least of all Faberge. Lynx sold like gangbusters, God knows.

YOU ARE MY KIN, GIRL

Let's consider three of the most heralded campaigns of the last fifteen years, big winners all of them in the marketplace and at Cannes. The first, for Maxell, won the Grand Prix in 1990. It showed a young Eng-lish tough, with a leather jacket, spiky hair, and an armful of cue cards. The soundtrack was from "Into the Valley" by the punk band the Skids. As the song played, the fellow danced in place while turning the cue cards one by one, "translating" the difficult-to-register lyrics:

> *Into the valley*
> *Peas sure sound divine.*
> *Sissy suffered you*
> *But who can viv iron?*
> *The soldiers go marching*
> *There's masses of lamb.*
> *Whose disease is cat skin?*
> *The picture in Hugh's toe*
>
> *Ahoy, ahoy, Len see a sty.*
> *Ahoy, ahoy, barman and soda*
> *Ahoy, ahoy, juicy men embalmed her.*
> *Ahoy, ahoy, lung nearly gave.*

It was hilarious—not because the Skids' lyrics were weird but because, as a viewer gradually came to realize, the transcription was so screwed up. "Whose disease is cat skin . . . *Juicy men embalmed her*"??? Nobody would write "Juicy men embalmed her," for crying out loud. That was the point. The guy had it all wrong. Ostensibly, it was a gag about how this bloke couldn't be sure of his accuracy, because he hadn't heard the song on Maxell audiotape. But the comedy was rooted in the famous unintelligibility of rock lyrics. (Your correspondent, for example, for many years remembered a Herman's Hermits lyric as "Seven days of the week, baby juicebone," when, in fact, the line was "Seven days of the week *made to choose from.*" Likewise, until very recently, I thought the Archies' big hit went "Sugar, aw honey, honey. You are my kin, girl, and you got me wantin' you." Truthfully, I was puzzled about why a rock band consisting of cartoon characters would be singing about incest. But finally, after more than thirty years of confusion, I was informed by my then-thirteen-year-old that the lyric was "You are my *candy* girl. . . .") And those are two bubblegum groups. Acid and metal and punk are even more obscure.

For the record, by the way, the Skids' actual verse was as follows.

Into the Valley
Betrothed and divine
Realizations no virtue
But who can define
Why soldiers go marching
Those masses a line
This disease is catching
From victory to stone

Ahoy! Ahoy! Land, sea and sky
Ahoy! Ahoy! Boy, man and soldier

Ahoy! Ahoy! Deceived and then punctured
Ahoy! Ahoy! Long may they die

Ah, an antiwar song. Who knew? Should've listened on Maxell tape.

Now then, another example: Exactly ten years later the Grand Prix at Cannes went to an odd and lovable campaign for Budweiser beer. It featured four friends, hanging around their various apartments, on a Sunday afternoon. They stayed in touch on the phone, in conversations limited pretty much to two words: "What's up?" Except they didn't say "What's up?" What they said, in increasingly elongated enunciations, was "Whassssssuuuuuup?!" The characters were all black, and the gag was rooted in a playfully, self-consciously exaggerated spasm of "black English."

Six months earlier, when the campaign broke, I'd given it three out of four stars in my column, explaining, "The 'AdReview' staff, the single whitest enclave outside of Latvia, doesn't quite get it but suspects it is very funny . . . with big catchphrase potential."

Well, I was right, and I was wrong. "Whasssup?" was indeed funny. In fact it was so funny it soon found itself on the lips of every able-bodied male American above the age of four. It was certainly worthy of more than three stars. Furthermore, I came to understand, the "Ad Review" staff is not the whitest enclave outside of Latvia.

The Cannes International Advertising Festival is the whitest enclave outside of Latvia. There are Klan meetings with more racial diversity (albeit inferior dining). Yet, all over Cannes for a solid week in June 2000, delegates of every nationality, language, and culture thrust their tongues out of their mouths and exclaimed/retched, "Whasssup?" There was no Latvian delegate present, but two Finns performed it for me in stereo in the Hotel Martinez with no prompting and no more than eleven cocktails apiece. So, yeah, *here's* what's up: the ad wasn't just some goofy inside-black-culture joke but a universal expression of eloquent male inarticulateness. What women can do with smiley, sympathetic head nodding men do with an ostensibly perfunctory greeting. These aren't mere words and gestures; they are bonds of understanding.

"Whasssup?" didn't mean "Pray, have you any news you'd care to impart?" It meant "You are my friend, and if you are doing anything interesting—interesting being defined as watching football and swilling beer—I'm in favor of doing it together."

So—unlike, say, Miller Lite's "Dick" campaign—this advertising absolutely understood its target audience. Furthermore, in the roles of Everymen, director/star Charles Stone and his friends were wonderful—especially the director himself, who wore something close to a Kabuki scowl of blank sports-viewing concentration until the "Whasssup?"'s started to fly, whereupon he became animated and charismatic. Furthermore, it all took place minus the obvious, and often vulgar, "Man Show" sort of jokes.

Furthermore, it was simply irresistible.

That's what turned the tide in the jury voting. There reportedly was some dissension among those who recognized the campaign's parallels to a then-three-year-old Brazilian campaign for Brahma beer, which also had football watchers on the phone—not gargling "Whasssup?" but enigmatically hissing "Tsssssssssss" (which turned out to be the sound of a Brahma beer being popped open). No problem, however. "Whasssup?!" sailed to the Grand Prix.

Finally, there was the famed Energizer bunny. I remember the first time I saw this campaign the way I remember the JFK assassination. The year was 1989. I was in Tupelo, Mississippi, birthplace of Elvis, watching TV in a nondescript Hilton. On the screen came a commercial for Nasatene Mist, some nasal decongestant. The spot began with some suffering wretch on his lawn, sniffing flowers his daughter had brought him and moaning, in misery, "Oh, my sinuses!" Then came the obligatory lab-coated presenter flogging the advertised product: "Only Nasatene has Muconol, the patented. . . . "

Oh, please. I lay there in bed, snorting at the cookie-cutter construction of the commercial. The brand was new to me, but the format was so familiar it was as if it were bolted together on some patent-medicine-ad assembly line. "I can't believe people get paid to produce this crap," I said to myself. Next thing I knew, a pink, drum-whacking Energizer bunny intruded on the scene and walked straight across the fake "Nasatene" spot, "going and going."

I'm not certain, but I'm pretty sure this was the first time I gave a television commercial a standing ovation. Yes, me, in my underwear, standing on my bed—my taut sinews rippling, excessive hotel-room ventilation blowing heroically through my hair, my $17 room-service pizza bobbing on the mattress like a speedboat in light chop—applauding and hooting with approval. Because it was brilliant. Because it was unexpected. Because I, Mr. Pundit, had been so terrifically taken in. Bravo!

The admiration was short-lived, as the world of advertising mediocrity took me immediately from the sublime to the ridiculous. The next commercial was for a coffee called Tres Cafe. A thirty-something housewife was entertaining a visitor on a rainy day, remarking preposterously about coffee flavor. Such genius, followed by such mind-numbing banality. For the briefest of moments I'd believed that advertising actually had the capacity to soar, and here it was, in the very next ad, wallowing in the dullest cliché.

Then the bunny barged in.

Nuh-uh! Twice, in the space of twenty seconds, suckered! So, of course I resumed my hooting, paying very little attention to the next commercial for Château Marmoset wine. When I did register what was going on with it, though, once again I felt the sap of disgust rising at this blatant knockoff of the Orson Welles campaign for

Paul Masson Wines—a disgust once again interrupted, to my astonishment and my delight, by the pink, mechanical rabbit. So, yeah, Energizer played me for a fool three times running. The immediate upshot was a rare four stars in "AdReview." The long-term consequence was an advertising phenomenon yielding more than 115 commercials over a dozen years.

The campaign didn't win at Cannes that year, though, because of a bit of a scandal. The jury became aware of a similar ad, done three years earlier in the United Kingdom, for Carling Black Label beer. In that spot action from one commercial spilled into two subsequent fake commercials for fake products.

That's right: the creative conceit was identical. Never mind that the Energizer commercials were far better produced and that the joke was vastly more relevant to batteries ("Keeps going and going") than it ever was for beer. In fact, as we'll see more of in Chapter 3, in the Carling commercial the gimmick was merely a clever idea in search of a sponsor. In the Energizer campaign it was a perfect metaphor for the central selling proposition. No matter, though. The bunny was deemed too derivative of Carling and summarily eliminated from Grand Prix consideration.

So what did win that year? Maxell won. Which was interesting, because it was no less derivative than Energizer. The idea of a single, mute presenter flipping cue cards was itself lifted from *Don't Look Back*, a 1965 D. A. Pennebacker documentary on Bob Dylan. In the opening sequence Dylan stands camera-center, displaying the transcribed lyrics to "Subterranean Homesick Blues." Oh, well. Maybe the statute of limitations had expired. (Why look back?) Consistency of ethical principles has never been the advertising industry's strongest suit. In 1987, as a protest against apartheid, certain Cannes jurors put down their Moët flutes, stepped out of their $900-per-night hotel suites and into the Palais des Festivals to arbitrarily award zeros to all work from South African agencies, effectively blackballing all of those entries from the competition. Exactly a decade later, apparently unaware of the human rights record of the world's largest dictatorship, the festival was giving standing ovations to the China delegation. Outrage is a matter of convenience for this community, and, as someone once sang, you don't have to be a weatherman to know which way the wind blows.

By the year 2000, not only did Cannes so embrace "Whasssup?!" that it was prepared to disregard the precursor Brahma campaign; the jury also conveniently ignored the genesis of "Whasssup?!" The vignette didn't begin as Bud advertising; it began as a short film used as a spec piece by director Charles Stone. Someone from DDB saw the piece, a bell rang in his head, and the appropriation of the concept for his Budweiser client was the result. Not only was this not an original idea; it was stolen from itself.

Am I saying, then, that it, too, should have been disqualified? No, no, no, no, no. I am saying the opposite. I am saying that it was a worthy Grand Prix for all the reasons previously delineated. It was a perfect expression of a universal experience. It resonated with the target audience. It was unexpected. It was entertaining. It was catchy. It was in every respect great advertising. Who *cares* that it existed first as a spec film? Who cares that the Energizer bunny owed a great debt to Carling? The festival is supposed to honor creative achievement. All of these campaigns were creative achievements—which is not synonymous with "never been done before." Far from treasuring originality as the advertising value to hold most dear, there is really no point—most of the time—in getting hung up on it at all.

If advertising were science, scholarship, journalism, or art, yes, of course it would make a difference. In those endeavors the essence of the journey is to challenge established ideas, to explore the unexplored, to cross boundaries, to question everything. If advertising existed for the purpose of aesthetically engaging the viewer in pursuit of universal truth, if advertising were an end in itself and the expression of its creator were its essential purpose, the answer would be perfunctory: authorship means ownership. But for those clad all in black I have the most horrible news: advertising creatives are not artists, nor *auteurs*. They are businessmen—or at least they're supposed to be. Their job is not to explore the unexplored. It is to *sell* stuff. It is to find an engaging way to get the client's message across to a skeptical and sometimes hostile audience.

It is not to be original.

Why bow at that altar? Who cares about originality besides the originator? Where is it written that consumers respond to novelty in advertising? I'm telling you that the consumer couldn't care less. The church that agency employees should be attending is not the Church of Originality but the Church of Ingenuity—finding intelligent, understandable, and, yes, sometimes, previously owned solutions to what is fundamentally a communications problem. Whether the goal is brand image, brand meaning, brand identity, brand comparison, brand repositioning, or whatever, advertising is there to communicate. Nobody is hired to do something novel. Novelty, as often as not, is camouflage for inability to solve the problem at hand. The Energizer bunny wasn't brilliant because it was original. It was brilliant because it was right. I mean, if novelty turns you on, may I suggest the *Guinness Book of World Records*? I believe Underwater Bowling Ball Juggling is wide open.

IF OVID GOT ROYALTIES . . .

OK, there. Hold on. Settle down. This is not to propose willy-nilly plagiarism or derivation or even formulaic advertising. Nor is it in any way to diminish advertising novelty when the resulting document succeeds majestically as advertising. Volkswagen's "Lemon" and "Think Small" obviously represented an unprecedented way to sell an automobile. "1984" was an unprecedented way to sell a computer. "Just do it" was an unprecedented way to sell sneakers (as no previous athletic-shoe manufacturer had previously told prospective customers, in effect, "Why don't you just get off your fat ass?"). These were monumental achievements that owe their transcendence largely to the fact that such approaches had never been tried before. They didn't succeed because they were original; they succeeded because they were smart. But it would be disingenuous to suggest that the surprise of their concepts wasn't part and parcel of their impact.

Furthermore, none of the foregoing is to accept the simplistic notion that *every* idea has been done before, that "There is nothing new in the world," which is one of those truisms that nobody ever challenges in spite of its being patently false. Sure, there's always some nimrod who believes that in the sixteenth century Nostradamus predicted sheep cloning, the World Trade Center attack, and "Fear Factor." There's always a crank claiming that his great uncle Hezekiah basically conceived the magnet resonance imager in 1883 while delivering a calf. And, of course, just based on the conversations I've had with advertising people over the years, there are literally thousands of people who wrote or co-wrote "Think Small." Naive platitudes notwithstanding, the fact is that across the entire scope of human endeavor innovation is the lifeblood of progress.

On the other hand, derivation has always been a fact of creative life. Shakespeare, whom you will continue to see referenced a lot in this book, owed an enormous debt to Seneca, Plautus, Plutarch, Marlowe, Ovid, and the Bible. I don't know what the interest would be on that debt, but let's just say that if Ovid weren't dead, he'd be a very rich man.

This gets to the third and final reason I chose the opening von Bülow anecdote. The maestro's young protégé stole from everyone he could think of. In more contemporary times we recall that George Harrison stole the melody to "My Sweet Lord," Eddie Murphy stole the idea for *Coming to America*. Senator Joe Biden stole half of his presidential campaign speech. And, really, what commentator hasn't borrowed a trenchant quotation here and there? In point of fact, the von Bülow story? I stole *that*, from a volume titled *The Book of Anecdotes*, published by Little, Brown & Co. and available at a fine bookstore near you.

So don't even think of it as "stolen," because, after all, "stolen" is such an ugly word. Think of it as any self-respecting advertising person would: New and Improved.

APROPOS OF SOMETHING

In a moment: important lessons about advertising. First, however, I shall explain the purpose of all literature.

Writing is about meaning. From novels to nonfiction, Restoration drama to the latest Paramount release, it exists to be about something—though not necessarily what it is nominally "about"; I'm not discussing plot here, nor even a set of basic facts. I'm speaking of purpose. There has to be a reason for telling the story and a reason for its being told. That is the essence of literature, and because that essence is explained mainly by high school teachers of dubious merit using curricula of bizarre inaccessibility to distracted teenagers of certain indifference, it is understood by almost nobody. That's why when you venture the conventional wisdom "I don't go to the movies for a message. I just want to be entertained," you are sure to get nodding heads of agreement. That's also why such irredeemable pieces of crap as *Independence Day* and *Titanic* can be blockbuster hits.

But "message" has nothing to do with it. We live in a country where five-year-olds read Aesop's fables with righteous morals and may not touch literature again until, at age sixteen, being force-fed Nathaniel Hawthorne or some such heavily allegorical author, whereupon they are badgered into divining "what the author is trying to say." No wonder we're a nation of dullards. Who cares what the author is trying to say? The question is: what have we experienced? What in the story reflects back on us in a way that resonates inside us? How does it relate to our understanding of our universe, of our society, or simply of ourselves? In short, how is it relevant?

That's why high schools, in introducing the American novel, should ditch *The Scarlet Letter* and replace it with *Catcher in the Rye*—so when the teacher asks "What is the story about?" the kids can answer in two words: "adolescent alienation." Then they can marvel about how the angst Holden Caulfield suffers at his fancy, "phony" prep school is strikingly similar to their own feelings. Then, in an instant, they can understand the universality of human experience and how literature doesn't issue "messages" but lavishes on us stories and characters that give us insight into our flawed and tortured selves. So, yeah, the syllabus should start with J. D. Salinger. Then, if I were running things, right to Shakespeare, who suddenly wouldn't seem like gibberish. I mean, did you *read* those sonnets in the first chapter? For a deceased individual, he sure knows what makes people tick. As for Hawthorne, well, in terms of making literature exciting for teenagers, he'll keep 'til later. Much later. He'll keep 'til never.

All right, that covers literature. Advertising, of course, has no responsibility to strike chords of shared humanity. (Although sometimes it does so very well. For more than twenty years, for instance, McDonald's commercials have plumbed the relationship between parents and little kids, delightfully capturing the joy/exasperation of reckoning with the four-year-old mind. Lots of terrible advertising is terrible because it aspires to be arty. Leo Burnett and DDB over the years have created a sort of art by doing nothing more than trying to sell hamburgers.)

If you think about it, advertising is the reciprocal of literature. It, too, must be *about* something, but unlike art it has the responsibility to convey an explicit message pretty nearly 100 percent of the time. Just as allegory is a small subset of literary writing, artistic merit—McDonald's or (I'm sure you'd prefer) "1984"—is a small subset of advertising. In this business, and please don't forget that it is a business, the message is the thing. That message can be about what benefits the brand confers, what image it projects, what values it embodies, what problem it solves. One way or another, every ad must—not *should* but *must*—resonate with the target consumer. That's its job. McDonald's genius in that regard is twofold, because we warm to seeing adorable vignettes about, say, preteens gossiping in the back of the car or Christmas shopping at the mall or being awakened by a toddler at 4:00 a.m. to go for a Happy Meal, and credit the advertiser for understanding our lives, but mainly because such little stories realistically perpetuate the basic selling premise that a McDonald's visit with kids has a magic in its own right—which, sadly, is true.

You don't need to be doing poignant slices of life, however, to worry about meaning and relevance. If sending a message is your principal mission, there are infinite possibilities for getting that mission accomplished, from hard-sell to gentle humor to in-your-face humor to product demonstration to sentiment to jingle jangling. It makes little difference, in general, which path you choose, as long as the path is reasonably straight and unobstructed. Just as there must be a message, there must be a clear-cut relationship between the message and the messenger. That responsibility cuts across all genres.

Unfortunately, a disturbing percentage of advertising these days is utterly compromised by *ir*relevance: "great ideas" assigned, more or less randomly, to the first client willing to buy them; celebrity presenters who bring nothing to the discussion but a famous face; extravagant digital effects employed not to solve a storytelling problem but for their own sake; funny, funny, funny gags appended for no apparent reason, apart from sheer entertainment value, to elusive, or nonexistent, selling messages. It's a pestilence. A *pestilence*, I tell you. And the exterminators seem to be asleep at the . . . at the . . . (I was going to say "switch," but that's a railroad metaphor that clashes with my vivid bugs analogy, which I am not prepared at this time to abandon. As I can't really think of where exactly exterminators are apt to doze on the job, I think I'll just drop the imagery for the moment and tell you about Manny and Sol.)

THE MEMORY JOKE

Manny and Sol, now retired, have been friends since they were kids. One day Manny drops in on his friend. "Manny!" Sol says. "How are you?" Manny shakes his head. "Solly, not so good. It's my memory. It used to be fantastic. Used to be, I'd see someone I did business with, I'd know his name, his middle name, his wife's name, their kids' names, birthdays, anniversary. Now I see someone I've known for thirty years, and I can't remember his name. It's so embarrassing. And so frustrating."

Sol patted his friend consolingly. "Manny, I know just what you're talking about. I had the same problem. Terrible. But I go to see this doctor. He has some sort of crazy system—symbology, association, I don't know what you call it. All I know is my memory's as good now as it was when I was twenty-five years old."

"Well, hell, Sol," Manny says, "I'll try anything. What's this doc-tor's name?"

Sol winces. "His name? OK, his name. . . OK, I'm thinking of a plant, flowering plant. Long stem. It's got a beautiful bloom—red petals, gorgeous red petals. And the stem, it's got thorns up and down it . . . a rose! Yeah, a rose. Rose. Rose." Then Sol turns and shouts toward the kitchen.

"Rose! What's that doctor's name?"

That's one of my favorite jokes. When I tell it, I give Sol a slight Yiddish dialect, which for some reason makes it even funnier. Plus, when you tell it in person, you get to do a little pantomime with the rose description that really adds to the whole experience. I heard it about eight years ago from a guy named Doug Berman, who tells it very well, but—in all modesty—not nearly as well as I do.

OK, so where was I?

Oh, yeah: more than one way to send a message. I remember now. Well, since humor so dominates advertising worldwide, we may as well start there. And where better than Federal Express?

Director Joe Sedelmaier's classic Federal Express work for Ally & Gargano in the 1980s was hilarious. Whether it was the fast-talking man, John Moschita, having four phone conversations at once, or any of Sedelmaier's trademark put-upon losers unable to get a package promptly from point A to point B, FedEx advertising was always laugh-out-loud funny. It was also absolutely, positively impos-sible to miss the message: via Federal Express, your package *will* arrive tomorrow. Every frame of every ad was about the value, to the target audience, of that service.

The equally classic Hamlet cigars campaign from Collet Dick-inson Pearce, London, was about poor schnooks whose worlds were perpetually collapsing around them. The funniest, and most famous, had a ridiculous little guy in a photo booth, trying vainly to manage his extravagant comb-over for a handsome self-portrait. But the camera always flashed at the wrong instant, catching him unposed. What did that have to do with cigars? Nothing and everything—because the ad, nominally about the frustrations of the photo booth, was actually about how, in a cruel, undependable world, one thing you can always count on is the postdisaster relaxation of a Hamlet cigar.

In 2001 there was a commercial for Heineken titled "The Pain Barrier." It showed a guy at a party, digging through an ice-filled barrel for a beer, discarding cans of ordinary domestics until, finally, after twenty agonizing seconds, he came up with a bottle of Heineken. With his prize clenched in his frozen extremity, he joined his pals, whose hands were similarly frostbitten. Like most observational comedy, it was funny because it required no further explanation. Every import drinker can, in a word, relate.

These spots exemplify one very good reason humor has become the default solution for ad-message communication. Whether to dramatize business needs or to suggest a modest remedy for feelings of victimization or to validate the notion that pricier beer is worth the sacrifice, each ad managed to be relevant to the audience it sought to impress, in a way calculated to be both entertaining and memorable. So much great advertising has done the same thing: "Speecy Spicy Meatballs" for Alka-Seltzer, "Got milk?" for the California Fluid Milk Processors Board, "The most wonderful time of the year" for Staples, "Funeral" for Volkswagen, "An elephant never forgets" for Rolo candy, "Where's the beef?" for Wendy's, "Tollbooth" for New York Lotto, and "Into the Valley" for Maxell audiotape. Then there's the magnificent, laugh-out-loud funny "This is SportsCenter" campaign for ESPN from Wieden & Kennedy, Portland, Oregon, which achieves relevance with humor by employing exactly the same jokey irreverence in its fake-documentary ads that uniquely characterizes its daily sports-news programming.

The problem is, nowadays ad agencies spend so much time and client money contriving to be entertaining and memorable that they skip the relevance part entirely. That gets to the long list of very *bad* reasons for the current comedy pestilence.

Like moths in the pantry, they are everywhere, these comic commercials. Everywhere and all the time and spreading—*not* like pestilence, come to think about it, but like disease. Like influenza or pink eye. (Only, you know . . . funnier.)

Not that there's anything wrong with funny TV commercials, per se, but, first of all, where is it written that you have to joke your way into the consumer's consciousness? Many important and persuasive documents have been penned over the centuries with no punch lines whatsoever. The Magna Carta. The Gettysburg Address. The Bible (although, the Book of Job . . . you know, at some point you've just gotta laugh). Add to that list of the nonhilarious, by the way, most of the best advertising ever created. As things stand now, though, a commercial pod on TV is a series of comedy blackouts, some funnier than others, but all at some point beginning to run together, depriving all of them of the very memorability that ostensibly commended the humor solution to begin with. But I guess it's easier to win trophies by being the funniest guy in the room. And maybe it's the best way for the all-in-blacks to deal with what I have long suspected to be their institutional self-loathing. The funnier their commercials are, the better they can persuade themselves—in spite of their nagging doubts—that they aren't mere Madison Avenue hacks flogging useless crap for Philistines, but comic artists capable of entertaining millions.

The fact is, there should be no shame in the profession (see Chapter 10, "Go Forth and Advertise"). But if creatives do have guilt feelings, multimillion-dollar ad campaigns are an extremely expensive way to purge them. On the client's dime, of course. God bless

Goodwill Industries, but the biggest underwriters of occupational therapy in the world are surely the Leading National Advertisers.

AND NOW A NON SEQUITUR FROM OUR SPONSOR

Here's a splendid example: a spot running in the United Kingdom at this writing, from McCann-Erickson, London, about three brothers obsessed with their Afro hairdos. One of them uses spray-on hair to cover his bald spot, which gives him an idea. Why limit Afro-ness to his head? So the guys, all dressed in goofy seventies fashions, spray the stuff on the roof of their old Ford and give it a bunch of little auto Afros. Then they go through a car wash, transforming the bushy little Afros into one gigantic car Afro. The voice-over: "That's what I call full-flavor behavior." The advertiser: Nescafé.

Nescafé. The instant coffee. Are you beginning to see my point?

Now, what I'm about to do is probably not fair, because an even more superb example of the phenomenon happened to be created by one of the consistently smartest and most able—and, by the way, funniest—agencies anywhere: Goodby, Silverstein & Partners, San Francisco. We wouldn't want them to get smug, though, would we, so permit me to confront them with one of their rare inexcusable boondoggles.

The campaign, from 1999, was for Sutter Home Winery. One spot, advertising cabernet sauvignon, showed a winemaker so absorbed in examining the Sutter Home grapes that she failed to notice federal agents rushing through vines behind her to apprehend a space alien, a leprechaun, and Sasquatch. Another, for merlot, showed a Sutter Home winemaker walking through the vineyard and among oak barrels, bemused by the delicate complexity of his product. This spot had absolutely all of the category's compulsory elements: the dramatic, smoky sunlight, the slow-motion photography, the mellow bed of strings and piano evoking "entrancing." A dead-on parody—paid off by the fact that the winemaker was so distracted that he was wearing his underpants outside his trousers. Then, in the third spot, a Sutter Home viticulturist labored in his lab as a TV behind him blared with the news headlines: "Good evening. Here's what's happening. The moon has just exploded. More on that amazing story later. And in medical news, two men have successfully switched heads. They're in good spirits and resting comfortably. And a local resident was attacked by angry squirrels. We must warn you: this footage is graphic."

The wine guy, of course, never flinched, because, as the superimposed tag line explained, this company is "way too focused on the wine." Then the voice-over: "Sutter Home. Preoccupied since 1890."

Pretty hilarious, no? Also completely, wildly, and insanely inappropriate.

If Sutter Home—which sells extremely low-end varietal wines—has any overarching mission in its advertising message, it is to persuade consumers that even at $5 this is quality wine. Maybe it's a beginner's wine or maybe it's an everyday wine, but it isn't jug wine. It's genuine. It's varietal. It's serious. That mission doesn't necessarily demand invoking all the clichés that the underwear ad so brilliantly parodies. It does mean, however, not using gags—no matter how hilariously memorable—that undercut any claim to seriousness you ever had. Though the tag line claimed "Way too focused on the wine," the message was exactly the opposite. Not only irrelevant but actually contrarelevant.

As I said, superb examples, but by no means the defining examples. The defining example, the quintessence, the apotheosis is the "Must Be Football Season" campaign—fresh, funny, delightful TV commercials about the country's peculiar autumn fixation. At least a dozen spots over several years have depicted ordinary Americans in ordinary situations that suddenly go haywire when something happens that reminds folks of football. My particular favorite is set in a shoe store, where the salesman is kneeling in front of a customer, holding a brown pump upright while reaching around for the other shoe. A second customer spies the hold, approaches, and boots the shoe soccer style for three points. Her defiant glower as she backs away from her placekick, arms raised, is simply priceless.

It's a perfect comedic gem, a thirty-second gift of laughter from our good friends at . . . Southwest Airlines?

Yes, Southwest *Airlines*, courtesy of GSD&M, Austin, Texas. And I'm grateful. Really, I am. The spots are a hoot—albeit a little, I don't know, air-travel-unintensive? All right, a *lot* air-travel-unintensive; they have nothing to offer about air travel whatsoever. What's especially bizarre is that Southwest is one of the few competitors in a mainly generic category with something newsworthy to say. They run a cattle car, but it's a very friendly and organized cattle car, and the prices are phenomenal. Furthermore, the concurrent Southwest campaign—"You are now free to move about the country"—is absolutely top-drawer. Yet not only do the NFL spots refuse to be so crass as to highlight Southwest's extraordinary Unique Selling Proposition they deftly avoid even the slightest reference to the brand, the category, or travel in general. The "Must be football season" campaign is thus the purest advertising example ever of utterly gratuitous entertainment value.

Alas, hundreds—if not thousands—of commercials are produced every year vying for the crown. Even though most of them aren't all that funny to begin with. Even though they are an abuse of the client's money and trust. Even though the viewer often can't remember the advertiser. Even though irrelevance, over time, is actually an irritant to viewers, who don't like to be left wondering why they've experienced what they've just experienced. Such as that Manny-and-Sol joke, for instance, coming to you out of nowhere for no apparent reason. No *apparent* reason. As a vivid example of charming-but-pointless entertainment, the memory joke does, at least—1,818 words later—make its point.

MICHAEL JORDAN 2: THE FIASCO

So, listen to this: You may not realize that, in addition to being the Apostle of Advertising Righteousness, I have a parallel career on public radio going as far back as "Ad Review." That's how I met Doug Berman, who told me the memory joke. Doug's the creator of "Car Talk" and "Wait, Wait, Don't Tell Me" on NPR. My show is called "On the Media," but before I got the cohost gig on "OTM," for years I was a commentator and roving correspondent for "All Things Considered." (So, yes, I *am* on a first-name basis with Andrei Codrescu, OK?) Anyway, back in 1996, I worked on a piece about going to Nashville to write a country song—which I did, in collaboration with a then-obscure songwriter named Rivers Rutherford, who is now a top Nashville writing star. ("Ain't Nothin' 'Bout You," "Smoke Rings in the Dark," etc.) Our song was titled "Tag, You're It," and it was supposed to embody traditional country themes plus my own Washington, D.C., inside-the-Beltway sensibilities. The song was about being so busy and supposedly important that you wind up playing telephone tag with your own gal, and I was very pleased with it but got the cold shoulder from a Nashville record exec and was flying back home to Washington with my tail between my legs when who should I sit next to but former president Jimmy Carter! The president—the living intersection of the Beltway and "Mayberry RFD"— loved my song and hooked me up with a friend of his to record it, which this fellow did, especially for my NPR broadcast, and oh, by the way, the dude's name was Willie Nelson.

And therefore, in the glow of such celebrity, you suddenly credit me more for understanding advertising, eh?

No, of course you don't. One thing has nothing to do with the other. Clearly, that whole passage—like the Manny-and-Sol story— was an utter non sequitur. A misdirection. A distraction. Apropos of nothing. Obviously, just as there is no relevance between football season and Southwest Airlines, there is no relevance between the enormously big names I can drop at a moment's notice and the merit of my advice about TV commercials. That's obvious to me, obvious to you, and completely lost on the clueless majority, who can't seem to grasp that the magic of celebrity appeal vanishes if the celebrity's image doesn't, at a minimum, square with the image of the brand being advertised.

The Charles Barkley/Hyundai debacle, for example.

Once again, it's no great mystery what motivates people to hire, say, a six-foot-nine multimillion-dollar basketball-playing jerk to front for the then-tinny-and-tiny cars. He was famous, an on-and-off-the-court personality, imbued with all the "stopping power" advertisers look for to keep viewers from clicking to another channel when the commercial comes on. Plus, at the time he was hired, he was probably the second-most-famous basketball player in the world. The most famous was Michael Jordan, far and away the most successful celebrity endorser in history. Lending his name to Nike, the man who came to be called "Air Jordan" first promoted a brand, then became transmogrified into it, then brand-extended *himself* to nearly single-handedly turn the modest sneaker business into a multibillion-dollar industry worldwide. The air pockets built into Nike's shoe soles for cushioning and (implied) greater leaping power coincided entirely with Jordan's own gravity-defying aerobatics, and the rest is marketing history.

Sometimes the marriage between product and presenter is just so perfect. Wendy's founder, Dave Thomas, square and old-fashioned himself, was such an ideal pitchman for Wendy's square and old-fashioned burgers that he overcame predominantly dreadful copywriting and his own intermittent on-camera deficiencies to become among the most successful and beloved product spokesmen in history, God rest his plain-speaking soul. Catherine Deneuve was the ideal front woman for Chanel No. 5 not because she was so extraordinarily beautiful but because she was so extraordinarily beautiful and *elegant*—which elegance happens to be the essence of No. 5's sophisticated appeal. Pamela Anderson is pretty well slapped together, too, but would look pretty silly next to a bottle of Chanel. Kind of like Eleanor Roosevelt looked pretty silly next to a stick of Good Luck margarine, and like Charles Barkley—fame or no fame—looked silly next to a Hyundai.

In fact, not just silly. Preposterous. As in not to be believed.

It is very bad when you spend millions and millions of dollars not to be believed. The fact is, however, when an advertiser trots a celebrity out there who creates cognitive dissonance with the brand he or she presumes to endorse, the stopping power is imposed not on viewer attention but on viewer credulity. Not only does it become painfully obvious that the famous face has been purchased for the occasion, but the viewer stops seeing the face altogether and sees only the transaction—which reflects well on nobody. Charles Barkley, minus the enormous check, wouldn't have sat his enormous butt anywhere near a Hyundai, and everybody knows it. While this campaign was on the air, Hyundai showrooms were the loneliest places in the world.

Yet it happens all the time: celebrities cast not in support of an advertising idea but in place of an advertising idea, living embodiments of poverty of imagination. And I'm not afraid to name names.

And I will. Right now.

Although that isn't as easy as it sounds, because such advertisers are more or less by definition forgettable, aren't they? So, uh . . .wait a second . . . *Hey, Rose, what was that sponsor's name?*

Oh, yeah: Samsung.

In 1998, Samsung Telecommunications of America, via the Arnell Group, New York, brought together a whole host of familiar faces from the celebrity "B" list. Joan and Melissa Rivers, Dr. Ruth Westheimer, MTV host Daisy Fuentes, and—perhaps because Charles Nelson Reilly was not available—Dom DeLuise.

Joan "Can We Talk?" Rivers was the only one among them with any apparent relationship to the product, which was cell phones. Dr. Ruth, of course, was over long ago but persists in the public eye like a recurring sty. As for DeLuise, well, that's what happens when summer stock is over and "Hollywood Squares" isn't calling. Not to say Samsung should eschew celebrities, but the minimum requirement is (ahem) A CLEAR CONNECTION between personality and product. Bob Newhart would have been nice. Dr. Laura Schlessinger. Hell, even the Jerky Boys. These are people we think of as using a telephone.

It gets worse, too. In 1998, Tommy Hilfiger, the sporstwear designer, and Deutsch, New York, hired comedian Michael Richards—for God knows what reason and at God knows what cost—to dress in drag for a thirty-second Super Bowl ad. A thirty-second, $1.6 million Super Bowl ad. About 100 million people saw it; not a single living being got it. In 1997, via Earle Palmer Brown, Philadelphia, Dollar Rent a Car acquired the services of the formerly amusing Chevy Chase. The scene of his first commercial appearance was an airport, where Chase, in the role of a businessman greeting three Japanese clients, had just rented a car. "Bonjour!" he said. Then, bowing in greeting, he banged his forehead against a client's forehead. (Of *course* it's hilarious, but try to catch your breath. There's more.) Later he would have raw octopus slip from between his chopsticks, trip over three golf bags, and down one of the visitors with an errant tee shot—proving that, despite all previous evidence to the contrary, Chase's talk show on Fox wasn't his career low point after all. It is simply hard to describe how soaringly, thunderingly, crashingly stupid this campaign was. Dollar Rent a Car called him "surf proof." Hah. He was a waxed board on a tubular breaker. The advertiser finally ditched him two years later, but for the agency, which lost the account, it was a day late and a Dollar short.

Don't take me wrong here. This has nothing to do with how highly I myself value certain celebrity talents. For example, I think *This Is Spinal Tap* is one of the funniest movies ever made, but I was appalled at the decision by IBM, via Ogilvy & Mather Worldwide, New York, to feature the fake heavy-metal rockers in a commercial aired during the 1996 Olympic Games. And nothing against the Olympics, either, which are full of drama and TV featurettes. But whereas I personally chuckled appreciatively at the casting, millions of others said, "Huh?" The "Solutions for a Small Planet" campaign thus became Solutions for a Small Minority, an elaborate, expensive in-joke.

On the plus side, the folks at Ogilvy got to meet Harry Shearer and Michael McKean, recognized by *Tap* aficionados as gods of comedy—a fact that, I strongly suspect, is behind the lion's share of celebrity miscastings. Should you ever find yourself in the vicinity of a senior vice president of marketing who has retained celebrity talent for advertising, be sure to wear steel-toe shoes. The names, dropped in pitiful approximations of casual mention, come crashing down like falling anvils. "It's like Chevy says . . . You know, Chevy Chase. He's doing some stuff for us. Big name, but a *helluva* guy. Great with the crew. Great with my kids. And a three-handicap, by the way." This is an expensive way to impress your neighbor, the orthodontist. Better to have your company spring for retainers for the whole block and do straightforward advertising clearly stating how it offers the same new vehicles as the Big Rent-a-Car Three at much lower prices. As for the argument that the celebrity spokesman also shows up at conventions, distributor meetings, and internal retreats—big deal. If impressing the troops is your goal, an open bar and a stuffed goody bag will do the trick very nicely at a fraction of the price.

Unfortunately, every advertiser who brings in a top-flight entertainer or athlete thinks he has the next Michael Jordan, although the fact is he *never* has the next Michael Jordan. Ask Rayovac, which failed so miserably with its celebrity pitchman for the Rayovac Rechargeable line of batteries that it ended up going out of the business. And who was that celebrity, starring in commercials by FCB/Leber Katz Partners, New York?

It was Michael Jordan.

Have you forgotten? Maybe, because we tend to repress the things that are most painful, you entirely blotted out the battery episode. But, sure enough, in 1995, Michael Jordan, noted environmentalist, was shot in tight close-up explaining why Rayovac Rechargeables would save the planet. No doubt that everyone involved in the hire was recalling the miracle of Air Jordan. What Michael put up for Rayovac was an air ball, an absolutely disastrous exercise in borrowed interest. The focus on out-of-context Jordan was particularly egregious because Rayovac Corp. had technology that should have been attention grabbing itself. By squandering its budget and close-ups on Michael, the advertiser failed to sufficiently explain or exploit the renewability advantage. Rayovac soon gave up on the rechargeables business and ended its ties with Jordan.

If only they'd learned from his aborted minor-league baseball career: the man can't handle AA pitching.

STARE AT THIS DIAGRAM

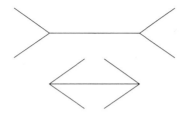

Which horizontal line is longer, the top or the bottom? Come on! They're both the same size! It's an optical illusion, y'nut ya! Isn't it great how the magic of Microsoft's Paint software enables me to surprise and confound you with unexpected bursts of computer-assisted wizardry?

And isn't it also great how I've remained true to the structure of this chapter, by once again—now for the third time—committing the very crime I'm about to dump all over when it occurs in advertising?

Just in case the point isn't clear enough already, the optical illusion—impressive display of computer applications though it may be—adds nothing to our discussion. It's the sixty thousand unforgettable words of text that give you gooseflesh, that excite your senses, that challenge your intellect, that touch your tender soul. As it happens, those words were crafted on the very same computer. You didn't think of them as computer generated, because how they were generated is totally invisible and beside the point. All you are concerned with is their staggering effect on your entire worldview—the substance, in other words, not the process. Advertising and advertising audiences are no different. The story's the thing. Everything else is irrelevant technology. The tools are important, and you have to know how to use them, but it's not about the tools. It's about the handiwork.

Like most common sense, unfortunately, that probably comes as news to most of the people who actually create advertising, especially car advertising. To sell BMWs, Fallon invested heavily in digital technology to turn the streets of New York into canals. To sell the Oldsmobile Aurora (remember the Aurora? remember Oldsmobile?), the Leo Burnett Co. invested heavily in digital technology to make the Statue of Liberty come alive. To introduce a new Honda, Rubin Postaer invested heavily in digital technology to have the little SUV negotiate the miraculously three-dimensional geography sprouting from the photographs in an outsize copy of *USA Today*.

These ads each cost a king's ransom to produce, and to what purpose? The best of the three was Aurora's, because the Lady-Liberty-as-King-Kong imagery was merely irrelevant to the product message. The other two spots actually undercut the product messages. The canals-of-Manhattan trick rendered the Ultimate Driving Machine into just another luxury boat, and the ostentatious off-roading-through-the-Life-section special effects were antithetical to Honda's longstanding theme.

"We make it simple," my eye.

Yet this stuff goes on all the time. A particularly favorite example of mine came from England in 2001. It opened with a lovely shot of a pear. Then, from nowhere, came a black-handled stainless-steel knife, flying directly into the fruit and dividing it. Because digital magic trumps physics, the knife didn't slow down. It continued on its destructive path, suddenly spinning like an arrow in flight, until it struck and pulverized a walnut. Then it shot through a bunch of white grapes, then it shattered a glass of Chardonnay, then it pierced a dripping glob of honey and then, finally, it burrowed into a hunk of cheese.

Grana Padano cheese. "Hits you with any flavour."

Huh?

Alternative idea, better and cheaper: hire Charles Barkley. Film him in his basketball uniform, dribbling up to a display of Grana Padano, carving off a slice, swallowing it, and saying, "Mmm. Take it from me, Charles Barkley. That's some damn fine cheese!"

Once again, don't get this wrong. I'm not saying technology has no place in advertising. On the contrary, it is indispensable. It's just a question of knowing what technology to deploy and when to deploy it. For instance, back in the car category, Jeep—via Bozell, Southfield, Michigan—has done one great commercial after another in which the digital effects have allowed the product to play the rugged outdoor hero. A recent one showed a rich couple at their big house after a day of off-road fun in their Grand Cherokee. Parked, covered with mud in their fancy driveway, the car began to shake itself like a wet Labrador, sending mud flying everywhere and, of course, revealing the refined luxury car residing within the trail-worthy beast. Very clever. The effect was complicated and expensive, but the message it permitted was worth the trouble and expense.

Better still: a 1998 commercial from DDB, Dallas, for Tabasco hot sauce. It showed a guy stuffing himself with pizza, which he was first liberally dousing with Tabasco. Next: a close-up of a mosquito attacking his arm. Then the mosquito flew away, only to explode in a tiny puff of pyrotechnics. This spot was so seamless in its use of whatever computer tricks it used that the viewer was unlikely even to notice it as a special-effects triumph. What the viewer noticed was a magnificent bit of visual hyperbole about the product attribute and the product attribute alone. In other words, it wasn't about cinema magic. It was about Tabasco.

AN ABUNDITY OF PROFUNDITY

A poem, by me:

> *Death and lilac, screaming. Aggrieved by the dawn. They*
> *Conspire, to the rage of heaven. Charred. Empty.*
> *Bleeding and gnawing for the want of a Song.*

Unspooling thunder awash in Lymph and daydreams.
Hell will not be undersold.

Pretty heavy, huh, how it just oozes with language and imagery and stuff? Notice, too, how bursting at the seams it is with the promise of high-toned significance—of which, I can assure you, it has none. I just now made it up, in about thirty seconds, to browbeat you yet again with the fourth major category of irrelevancy. As we have seen, it's easy to fall so in love with a joke or a special effect, or so in the thrall of a star, that you neglect the business at hand. Herewith another siren that creatives too often are drawn to, to the detriment of the mission: their own deep, deep, deep profundity.

Here again the "1984" Paradox rears its head. So devastating was that ad in establishing an instantaneous, trenchant, and enduring brand promise—the Macintosh as antidote to losing your soul—that successive campaigns for any number of advertisers continue to go to the (Or)well too often. How can you not be inspired by "1984"? Or—no matter that he is probably the world's most lethal serial killer—by the Marlboro cowboy, who defied every cigarette marketing convention by eschewing boasts about tobacco quality in favor of silently conveying individuality and rough-hewn serenity? And every so often a contemporary campaign, in embracing the values of brand meaning as opposed to practical brand benefits, pulls off the same miracle.

I'm thinking of a small but exceptional 2000 campaign from Fallon for PBS. The campaign was targeted mainly at the Public Broadcasting Service's existing audience, to remind them why public broadcasting exists and to flatter them about what kind of person tunes in. The obvious approach would have been to sample the network's rich variety of programs, the sort of programs that would never find purchase on commercial television. "Frontline," "Masterpiece Theatre," "Nova"—that sort of thing. The sort of thing that doesn't necessarily appeal to the viewers of, say, the Fox network, which broadcasts such nonmasterpiece theater as "Who Wants to Marry a Millionaire?" and "The World's Most Infected Animal Bites!" or whatever.

The PBS campaign came at a critical moment, after various mouth breathers in Congress had done their best to strangle "elitist" public broadcasting ("elitist" being defined by the Tom DeLays of the world as anything more sophisticated than "Walker: Texas Ranger"). PBS had been able to hold off the barbarians at the gate but was girding for another assault. This was all the more reason to trot out the evidence that, far from undermining national values, PBS is a national treasure. But Fallon didn't. What it did, magnificently, was remind its viewers that curiosity lives. Not the voyeuristic curiosity that informs the programming of commercial trash aimed at the basest common denominator, but the genuine desire to understand and more vividly experience the world around us.

One spot was about a little farm girl sneaking outside in the middle of the night with a spotlight, which she raises over the horizon of the henhouse window until the rooster inside, tricked, begins to crow. Another showed a little boy opening the dishwasher and removing a video camera, which is wrapped in a Ziploc bag. He'd taped the wash cycle to see how it works.

The true tour de force, though, was the third spot, which opened in a dime-store photo booth. Behind the curtain, a man sat mugging and gesticulating for one set of photo strips after another. At first it looked like an homage to the Hamlet Cigars spot, but, no; not hardly. Instead we got a second peek at him, silently emoting for the camera. Cut to scene two: the same guy, at home, cutting apart the photo strips and listening to Enrico Caruso's ancient RCA Victor recording of the aria "Di Quella Pira" from Verdi's *Il Trovatore*. Why? To staple the images into a flip book. Letting them fan through his fingers, he became the lip-synching star of a homemade opera nickelodeon.

Bravo! All three spots began nearly all in black, all but a circle of tightly closed aperture that widened to reveal the opening shot. It was a nice effect but also a perfect metaphor: open your eyes and a more interesting life awaits you.

So, yeah, sometimes counterintuitive ideas are brilliant ideas. More often they result in extravagant productions of no idea. Worst of all is what happens with even more astonishing frequency: when the Great Revelation reveals itself to be the wrong idea altogether.

"It's heard laughter, tears, secrets," said the gentle female voice-over to open a 2000 commercial, atop a montage of home-movie images and snapshots from the fifties and sixties. "It knows the sound of concern, of joy, and of regret. It's heard about movies, books, school, and boyfriends—and, at times, simply heard nothing at all."

Hey, nice writing, from WestWayne, Tampa, Florida. A little gooey, but nice. At this stage viewers began to understand that all of these warm and precious moments are indigenous to one very special place: the kitchen. The birthday parties, the family meals, the hugs, the arguments—everything the images portrayed happens at family life's ground zero. Who can't relate to that? The emotional resonance of the venue having been established, the voice-over returned to make a proposition: "If only there were a place that made you feel the way you did at your kitchen table." An inviting thought. If only. If only there were such a magical place. "Maybe there is," the onscreen type supposed. Then came . . . the Denny's logo.

Denny's??? Yes, the home of "$1.99! Are you outta your mind?" was claiming to be America's Kitchen Table—which, um, it is not. Could Kraft Foods invoke that imagery? Sure. Betty Crocker? Absolutely. Wonder Bread? Why not? They all have a legitimate claim to the extremely potent emotion invested in a few square feet of precious floor space two strides from the fridge. With Denny's, though, the association simply didn't scan. It was a total disconnect. In some ways Denny's is the *anti*–Kitchen Table. When families gather there, it is most often for an occasion, or a rest stop, but certainly not for the routine of day-to-day life, except for the caffeine-starved rat racers who show up every morning for a hot mug of java and an egg or six.

The notion of the ad and the sentiment were ingenious and lovely. I'd seen nothing like it since 1993, when American Standard (and agency Carmichael Lynch, Minneapolis) spoke about bathtub hardware by reminding you, "It's seen you naked. It's heard you sing." Turning an inanimate object into a witness of your most intimate moments is undeniably clever. In the kitchen example the possibilities may have seemed even greater, so laden with emotion is the family-life tableau. But that doesn't change the fact that Denny's does not and cannot intrinsically qualify for the honor.

But that's nothing. Go back to 1995. Somebody has a chilling, cautionary message for you. Get out the remote, power up the converter box, have a seat, and take it all in.

The scene is also vaguely Orwellian but apparently set in the present: a brooding apartment dweller on his way home from work through the dusky, sullen city. The man is tense, anxious, preoccupied. Passing a giant telescreen filled with images and buzzwords of the digital age, he glances upward with contempt. "I'm somebody," he says, in interior monologue. "I'm somebody. Have you thought about that when you're building this thing, this so-called superhighway? Have you thought about me? Listen to me. This revolution that's taking place, it's not about technology. It's about people. It's about us. Government, bureaucratic corporations—they're all alike, telling us what's right. Maybe that's what's wrong."

Dear God, what is the wretched soul fretting about? Technowar?

Dehumanization?

Soylent Green?

Nah. He's worried about cable. This claustrophobic vignette of anxiety, depression, and paranoia was brought to you by the Red Ball

Tiger agency in San Francisco for Tele-Communications, Inc., the world's largest owner of cable systems. The tag line: "We're taking television into tomorrow."

Yeah? What they should have been taking was this fellow into therapy. And that was the more cheerful of two spots. The agonized hero of the second commercial—fearing for his kids' future—looked positively suicidal. But TCI, presumably, was poised to save the day by understanding the power and potential of cable to guide the world, sensibly and sensitively, into the twenty-first century. The ads didn't specify, however, which particular portions of cable's offerings would come to the rescue. Would that be the Cartoon Channel portion? The home-shopping portion? The music-video portion? The porno-graphic-movie portion? It's like, yo, TCI: Skip the hyperreality and try to regain touch with reality itself.

On that subject, I'll leave you with the most infamous example of post-"1984" delusions of profundity. It came to pass in 1985, very specifically, because "1984" had been such an unexpected phenom-enon. It, too, was crafted especially for the Super Bowl, at a cost of $1.6 million, including airtime. (Remember, this was a long time ago, when $1.6 million was a substantial sum of money.) The message was quite similar as well, but this advertiser would have nothing like the experience Apple had had a year earlier.

It wasn't because the advertiser wasn't as smart as Apple. It wasn't because the advertiser wasn't as bold as Apple. It wasn't because the advertiser wasn't as profligate as Apple. The advertiser, in fact, *was* Apple. The commercial was titled "Lemmings." It por-trayed an endless trail of business-suited executives (think "IBM"), marching and singing "Hi ho! Hi ho! It's off to work we go!" The gai-ety was meant to be ironic, because, see, they were marching toward the edge of a cliff. And off they tumbled, one after another, into the sea, like lemmings. Get it?

Of course you get it. The Chiat/Day commercial, which was supposed to invite corporate users to be as independent thinking as the nerdy iconoclasts who favored Macintosh, had the subtlety of an exploding cigar. It had none of the drama and visual spectacle of "1984," and, as a bonus, it insulted the target audience. Mindless corporate automatons, it turns out, don't like being portrayed as mindless corporate automatons.

"Awful in its overstatement," declared Tom Shales of the *Washington Post*, and that was an understatement. "Lemmings" was profound, all right. It was a profound disaster. Shortly thereafter the agency, which only a year earlier had produced the greatest commercial in the history of advertising, lost the Apple account to BBDO.

So, there you are: four of the Five Great Irrelevancies. Here is where I stop, because the fifth gets a chapter all its own.

EXERCISE REGULARLY AND TRY CUTTING BACK ON THE SEX

Their eyes met.

Although not literally, because the corneal abrasion would have taken the white-hot glow off the passion then smoldering under the sofa cushions of their desire.

Strictly speaking, what met was their glances. Her irises were boiling cauldrons. His stare was a ravenous wolf, swallowing her whole. They glided across the room—he the lupine predator and she the extremely heavy iron pots of bubbling liquid—and fell into each other's arms. Or paws, or ladles, or whatever. Their hands grasped wildly. Their tongues searched for one another, taking no time at all, as there they were, dangling right there inside their mouths. The world around them disappeared as the pair transformed into Tesla coils of electricity, blue arcs of energy bristling all around them, creating an audible buzz of barely suppressed ecstasy. Plus, because this was allergy season, some nose whistling.

His magic siphon swelled like a proud mother. She was damper than a moist towelette, either the Wash 'n' Dri brand or the competing, popularly priced Wet Nap. All at once he lifted her. She gasped, threw her head back, and screamed.

It was a State of the Union address nobody would ever forget.

Hot yet?

Of course you are, because in addition to being a connoisseur of exquisite writing, you are also a human being, which means you are probably preoccupied with imagined sexual encounters all day long—except during sex, when, if you're a man, you're thinking about how long you'll be obliged to stay awake afterward or, if you're a woman, when you're ever going to get some decent sex.

A famous University of Louisville study tells us that teenage boys think about sex every second minute, girls every three minutes. Beaten down by the ravages of age and the world-weariness of experience, middle-aged men and women report thinking about sex only once every ten minutes. Which is six times an hour. Which is, let's say, ninety-six times per day—not counting sleeping, which is when those sexual thoughts often concern acts that, as the Louisville researchers are well aware, are felonies in the commonwealth of Kentucky. You yourself have had some pretty skanky ideas run through your head; that's a guarantee. (Individual perversions may vary. Void where prohibited.)

Now, obviously, this frequency-of-sexual-thoughts thing is one of those statistics people cite without having any idea whether, out of the context of a university psychology lab, it's actually true. The best we can do is determine whether it tracks with our own experience, and maybe flesh it out with some specifics. For that we turn to a 2001 Internet poll of AOL users, asking what makes them think about sex. Among the replies:

- a pretty woman
- a handsome man

- a pair of broad shoulders
- the glimpse of a bra line
- a hot bath
- love songs
- hearing the doorbell
- tanning
- TV movies
- magazines
- my cat

The doorbell, ladies and gentlemen. The *doorbell*. The point is that sex is a basic human instinct, right up there with fight or flight, satiating hunger, and hiding things from your mother. It is not only a staple of our daily thoughts but a recurring theme in art and literature since time immemorial and the single dominant influence on the popular culture, from Britney Spears to "Sex and the City" to Internet pornography. No surprise, then, that it is a staple in advertising as well. In fact it's more than a staple. It's the whole damn Swingline warehouse. There is scarcely a category in all of advertising—with the possible exception of, say, business-to-business promotion of telemarketing call-center technology—that hasn't invoked sexual imagery, sexual situations, or just basic sex appeal. This runs the gamut from your typical, fetchingly costumed hot babe in ten thousand beer commercials to a postcoital scene between an elephant and an ant to sell Tulipan personal lubricant in Argentina to an unforgettable Australian cinema ad, for a radio station, starring a singing penis. (Less offensive than you'd think, thanks to choreography accomplished with monofilament fishing line and digital effects allowing a convincingly rendered and extremely hilarious lip-synching urethra.)

So let's just say, as a starting point, that sex is a fixture in advertising because it inevitably *must* be a fixture in advertising. If the key to the business is winning the hearts and minds of target consumers, the most reliable route may well be through the gonads—which advertising sometimes can accomplish in the most provocative ways.

One of the great television-commercial masterpieces, directed by Ridley Scott in 1979 for Chanel No. 5, was a surrealistic, swimming-pool fantasy filled with fetching, implicitly erotic imagery, and impossibly gorgeous models but without one frame of graphic flesh-peddling or vulgarity. It was the perfect synthesis of sexuality and sophistication, as much a work of art as a piece of advertising. And one of the comic classics of advertising worldwide, from Norway for Braathens Safe Airlines, depicted a surprise lunchtime visit home by a randy husband. Imagining a bit of afternoon delight with the missus, our paunchy red-bearded hero undresses, sticks a rose between his teeth, and throws open the French doors to the living room, only to discover his wife enjoying tea . . . with her parents. They'd flown in unexpectedly on half-price Braathen Safe tickets. A strategically located teacup obscures our view, but the in-laws are treated to full frontal son-in-law nudity. The ad was as charming as it was funny and an improbable but vivid way of—if you will—fleshing out the excitement of spur-of-the-moment travel.

The problem, unfortunately, is that so much advertising sex is neither charming nor artful nor remotely to the point. Sex is employed so haphazardly, so excessively, and very often so abusively that it frequently does more harm than good. Think of it this way: salt improves the taste of almost everything, but too much salt also ruins almost everything, including your health—and it never tastes good on Jell-O. This chapter, therefore, is about how to use salt. The instruction will include a little bit of history, an awful lot of self-reflective talk therapy, and, naturally, some defining examples of why sex has its rightful, salty, nigh-unto-magical place in advertising. In the end, I expect, you will have a sound framework to make the right decisions, and you will appreciate the author for who I truly am: the living synthesis of Alan Alda, whose respectful sensitivity defined the liberated eighties male, and Popeye the Sailorman, whose eyes bug three inches out of his head when a beautiful goyl like Olive saunters by.

But fair warning. Unlike the indiscriminate use of humor, celebrities, special effects, and illusory Big Ideas, the abuse of sex in advertising does not hinge merely on relevance. There are also major issues of propriety and exploitation to be considered, issues that are not to be glibly tossed away. Much as I'd like to remain in the vein of fake bodice-rippers and comical, human sexual folly, no can do. When the subject of sex in advertising leads inexorably to the matter of sex*ism* in advertising, the stakes are too high for high jinks. For instance, prepare to be appalled: there was a cigarette ad, for the all-American brand Lucky Strike no less, that dramatized its "mildness" claim by depicting the kidnapping and presumed sexual assault of a half-naked woman, her bare breasts exposed as she was carried off bodily by two broad-shouldered thugs.

What? You don't remember any such monstrosity? Of course you don't. It's from 1933.

"Nature *in the Raw* is seldom *MILD*," the headline blared, hard by the artwork of a young woman being carried off by a pair of invading Norsemen in the A.D. 845 rape of Paris. The supposed connection to the brand: Luckies aren't raw; they're toasted for mildness. The actual message, beyond the transparent pretense of art and history: "Hey! Check out those bazooms!"

At the time, the new president was Franklin Delano Roosevelt. Yes, at the dawn of the twenty-first century, we are awash in sexual appeals, but don't imagine that the phenomenon is new. In fact, before exploring further the consequences of sexual imagery run amok, this would be a fine time to stroll down memory lane.

WHAT DID YOUR HAIRDRESSER KNOW, AND WHEN DID HE KNOW IT?

Here's what happened in 1911: The Triangle Shirtwaist Factory fire in New York City killed 146 sweatshop laborers. Roald Amundson reached the South Pole. Ray Harroun won the first Indianapolis 500, averaging 74.6 mph. Airplanes were first used as weapons during the Turkish-Italian War. Lillian Devere and Earle Williams starred in the unforgettable Hollywood blockbuster *Aunt Huldah, the Matchmaker*. The NCAA football championship was shared by Princeton and Penn. The seventh-most-popular name for newborn girls was Mildred. The tenth most popular was Ethel.

Oh, and one more thing. Sex in advertising was born.

Or not. There are those who argue that a 1491 Belgian woodcut announcing publication of *Histoire de la Belle Melusine*—and showing off a little woodcut flesh of *la* bathing *belle*—has a proper claim. But the document most widely credited for semiexplicitly baring the subject in semimodern advertising was for Woodbury's Soap. "A Skin You Love to Touch" was the headline. The model was quite attractive, and the implication was that the "you love" really meant "he'll love." (Wait a minute. Turkish-Italian War? *There was a Turkish-Italian War?* How can I worry about soap and sex when I seem to have misplaced an entire war? This is all so traumatizing. So let's skip the next quarter century.) Twenty-five years later, Woodbury's also would be credited with the first frontal female nudity in U.S. national advertising—credit awarded, apparently, on a technicality. The girl in the Lucky Strike ad was partially draped and more or less on her back. Either way, nothing has happened in the intervening time to stem the tide of "progress."

One of the most famous examples hails from 1957. Eisenhower was in the White House. The introduction of the birth-control pill was still three years away, so the vaunted Sexual Revolution hadn't quite begun. But there in women's magazines and such general-circulation titles as *Life* was the photo of a beautiful young mom, headlined with the provocative question "Does she . . . or doesn't she?"

Uh, does she or doesn't she *what?* The answer, ostensibly, was "dye her hair." Clairol was positing that its product was so natural-looking that "Only her hairdresser knows for sure." But, although copywriter Shirley Polykoff denied any intentional double entendre, the world leapt to other conclusions. In fact the reader could fill in the blank any which way, according to her own personal peccadillo, and the ad still scanned. As for the "hairdresser" payoff, that scanned, too. In the era before widespread psychoanalysis, Mr. Randy down at the salon was the trustee of all secrets. Not incidentally, 1957 was also the era before widespread use of hair coloring. Thanks to this campaign, and because advertising works, and because advertising that genuinely resonates with the consumer can perform astonishing wonders, by 1958, as Mr. Randy and the Clairol Co. well knew, "she" did.

Shortly thereafter, all hell broke loose. The Sexual Revolution did, in fact, begin, and erotic innuendo was everywhere. Not only were the variously coy and overt sex references not widely criticized; they were deemed daring and sophisticated. Hip. Trendy. Exhilarating. Very modern, adventure-wise. When a 1965 Braniff Airlines television ad featured one of its stewardesses stripteasing for male passengers, unfurling one item of Emilio Pucci fashion at a time ("The air strip is brought to you by Braniff International, who believes that even an airline hostess should look like a girl"), there followed zero fulminations of feminist outrage. In fact, Braniff ridership went dramatically upward.

The following year, the straitlaced packaged-goods shop called the William Esty Agency hired an eighteen-year-old blond model named Gunilla Knutson to shave a man on camera. The music track was the bump-and-grind standard "The Stripper," and Knutson's line was "Take it off. Take it *all* off." Knutson became the nation's preeminent fantasy girl. Sales of Noxzema Medicated Instant Shave Cream soared.

Another extremely popular spot from 1966 was for Diet Pepsi, titled "The Girls Girl Watchers Watch." It consisted of sixty seconds of women walking by and men gawking at them. The instrumental song—"Music to Watch Girls By"—was released as a single and sold big. And the idea of deploying women in TV commercials purely as sex objects looked better and better.

One glaring consequence was what Betty Friedan, in her watershed book *The Feminine Mystique*, called "progressive dehumanization." The apotheosis of Friedan's worst nightmare came in 1972 in a campaign for National Airlines. Copywriter Dick Wolf—who went on to fame as the creator of television's "Law and Order" series—thought it would be cute to feature gorgeous National stewardesses photographed with come-hither expressions and a beckoning call to action: "I'm Cheryl. Fly me." This odious euphemism finally drew blood. Flight attendants were so infuriated, some of them wore buttons on the job that said "Fly yourself."

For all the good that did. The next three decades produced an increasingly explicit, sometimes bizarre array of sexual images and references. In 1980 Calvin Klein put fifteen-year-old supermodel Brooke Shields on her back in a pair of tight, tight jeans, her hips thrust upward. "Know what comes between me and my Calvins?" she cooed. "Nothing." Parse the meaning any way you wish. This experiment with jailbait presaged two decades of Calvin Klein outrages, including two other episodes of thinly disguised kiddie porn.

In 1991, Sprite, the lemon-lime soft drink, provided what it called "an unexpected twist," about a blundering would-be novelist at his computer keyboard, vainly trying to pen the Great American Novel. When the literary loser's shrill, bosomy girlfriend annoyed him, he simply hit the "delete," and up in smoke the bimbo went. Poof! Soda-pop ad as snuff film. Which *was* unexpected—not sexy, but obscenely sexist, maybe the most misogynistic TV commercial ever aired.

In the same year, Dow Brands introduced a line extension called Fantastik Swipes, a two-sided wipe with one side soft, the other side coarse for scrubbing. This concept it communicated with two trios of bumping, grinding women—one trio blond, clad in white, the other brunette, clad in black leather. In other words, to promote a home cleaning product, principally to women, on daytime television, Dow Brands opted for the good slut/bad slut approach to making the sale. (Oddly, that product no longer exists.) On the other hand, beginning in 1998, and targeting approximately the same audience, Clairol played on the superficial similarity of the words *organic* and *orgasmic*. Ha. Ha. Ha. Women writhing and moaning in the shower, enjoying "a totally organic experience." Alas, that totally moronic campaign, for Herbal Essence shampoos, was an unqualified success. H. L. Mencken famously observed, "No one in this world has ever lost money by underestimating the great masses of the plain people," and he wasn't wrong.

So there's your history for you, and, yes, sex has always been everywhere, at least in its hypothetical form. And none of the foregoing is even to mention high-fashion print advertising, whose stock in trade is the depiction of stylized fetishism, and industrial trade advertising, which requires no product-related reason to focus on a model's overflowing cleavage. In fact, now that I think of it, a business-to-business provider of call-center technology for telemarketers called Cosmocom did, indeed, advertise with a cute blond spilling out of her tight cocktail dress. So I believe now every single category is covered.

But you never know. So, right now as I sit here, I'm going to try an experiment. Each month, I peruse a reel of fifty-three commercials compiled by a British company (stupidly) called Xtreme Information. The spots are selected from around the world based on what Xtreme deems to be the most interesting new work on the air. Suffice it to say this roster seldom corresponds with what I deem to be interesting. In any given month, by my lights, at least forty-five of the fifty-three spots are terrible. Not ordinary. Not mediocre. Terrible. Partly because what interests Xtreme is impact, not salesmanship, and partly because what interests most of the allegedly creative world is not salesmanship either. One thing that does interest both the world at large and its Xtreme microcosm, however, is sex. Lots and lots of sex ads in this reel month after month after month. And that's my experiment. I'm going to open the latest package right now, load the VCR with the January 2002 compilation reel, and scan it for sex-related ads. Then I'll come back and report on which advertisers felt the necessity of invoking sex to promote their goods and services and evaluate how they succeeded. OK? I'll be right back.

AND WAS THAT MAYOR McCHEESE IN THE HOT TUB?

All right, I'm back. And though I must admit the percentage of sex-related material is quite low this month relative to previous reels—eight spots out of fifty-three, as opposed to a typical fifteen or twenty out of fifty-three—the percentage of *relevant* sex-related material is right in line with the average. That is: zero.

Allow me to offer the evidence. From Argentina, we find a pretty young woman on a crowded bus. A young man squeezes her shapely butt. She swings around angrily, only to find a half dozen men, all looking equally innocent. But one guy is red-faced, so she hauls off and coldcocks him. Was he blushing out of guilt? No, because he didn't use his Banana Boat sunscreen to keep his face pale. So there you have it: never mind skin cancer. Always wear sunblock in case you are on a crowded bus and you are standing nearby when some pervert pinches a woman, lest you be mistaken for the perpetrator.

From Germany, a woman goes to an erotic masquerade ball. Adultery occurs. She comes home. Her husband gives her a Patek Philippe watch. (Takes a licking and keeps on ticking, I reckon.) From the United States, in a commercial for a prescription drug, women at a swimming pool stare at the hunky guy with the nice chest and washboard abs. Quite a hunk, yessiree, but he has a disorder the women cannot see. Is this ad for Viagra? No, it is for Lipitor, the cholesterol drug. Got it? Want to impress chicks? Get rid of that gross arterial plaque.

From the UK, a couple do the nasty in their bedroom, oblivious of the panel of Olympic judges observing and voting on their performance. This is for Holmes Place, a health club. The connection is that . . . never mind; there is no connection. From Argentina again, gorgeous people at a fancy party have their sexual fantasies materialize before our eyes. Most of them involve Gancia vermouth. That's right, Gancia, the *sexy* vermouth.

All of those spots invoked sexuality not because it corresponded with the product or the promise but because the people behind the advertising didn't have any real ideas. As is so often the case, attention getting was mistaken for a goal. But attention and awareness are secondary benefits; they should never be the goal. As the drunken party buffoon who puts the lampshade on his head knows only too well, attention doesn't in and of itself win friends. There is no point in getting everybody's attention if you have nothing to offer once you have it. What people do then is just nervously edge away.

This brings me to one more sex-centric spot from the Xtreme reel. It's from Singapore, and at length it follows the progress of a supremely unattractive man wending his way through the exotic dangers of a brothel, where a scary bevy of whores promise him something "hot and spicy." He gets it, too. He gets a hot and spicy . . . sandwich. Yes, it's a brothel vignette to sell a fast-food meal. And the advertiser?

McDonald's. I swear to God, and I have nothing further to add.

So, as we have seen, the indiscriminant use of sexual imagery, like the indiscriminant use of humor, special effects, celebrities, or whatever, is antithetical to the purpose of selling goods and services to people who might consider surrendering their money to you. And, again, there are some other sex-related risks, too, such as sexism and just plain rudeness (see Chapter 6, "Be My Guest"). But let me also reiterate that sexual content is sometimes just the right touch. I've named some famous examples. Let me describe one less prominent, but nonetheless compelling, from 1996.

It was a two-spot introduction, from Fallon McElligott, Minneapolis, of Lee Riveted Jeans. It was also—if you were spoiling for a fight—a brazen, unapologetic celebration of the shallowest kind of human interaction, shamelessly validating the display of body parts as instruments of seduction. The ads proclaimed, in essence, "Buy Lee. Show off your butt. Get lucky."

And they were delightful.

One was set in an apartment building laundromat, where a young woman glanced nervously at an overhead clock as she stuffed dollar bills in the coin changer, one after another. Entered then a nice-looking, Lee-clad guy making his way to the laundry, where he found the "empty" light blinking on the machine. "Excuse me," he said to the woman, "do you have any change?"

"Let me check," she coyly replied. Then the voice-over: "Lee Riveted. Cut to be noticed."

In other words, the Wonderjean.

The spot was shot in black and white, providing a vérité texture that enhanced its humanity and charm. So, too, the second spot, filmed in a coffee shop, where a scraggly, handsome Gen Xer loitered late into the night, drinking refill after free refill of java while gazing at the comely waitress as she strode away in her snug Lee jeans. Finally, at closing time, she asked, "Anything else?"

"No. Yes. Maybe," he stammered. "If you're not busy, maybe we can get a cup of coffee?" More coffee? She smiled. He winced. And no wonder. The mating dance is awkward, especially for those handicapped with language and reason. As Scott Russell Sanders observes in "Looking at Women," his seminal essay on the conflict between civility and sexuality, only human males—versus billy goats, for example—are self-conscious about how they gaze at the female of the species. But as Sanders also observes, "There is more billy goat in most men than we care to admit." And more nanny goat in women.

There's no faulting feminist anxiety about the degradation of women through objectification in advertising and elsewhere. And of course it's true that body worship is a superficial trivialization of core human values, values centered on character, personality, humor, intellect, moral strength, and mutual respect. Indeed, what distinguishes us as civilized beings is the ability to be governed by reason and inner sensibilities, not only by our animal desires. On the other hand, it's stupid to pretend we have no animal desires. It may be politically correct. It may be progressive doctrine. But it is also a fiction. Erase the influences of sexist culture and you are still left with the human animal, bristling with instinctive, glandular responses to the opposite sex that may have nothing whatsoever to do with character and everything to do with the shape of a bejeaned behind.

The Lee campaign conceded this point—no more, no less—without attaching a value judgment. It was a billy goat and nanny goat worldview, fabulously, soaringly, majestically incorrect. It was also truth, in black and white. Because nobody is buying Lee Riveted Jeans for the rivets.

So what better commercial to serve as a point of departure? The time has come to ruminate on the meaning of it all, to think this thing through. I mean that literally. It's easy enough for me to lay down the commandment. That's coming, believe me. But on this subject of sex (and only on this subject), I beg your indulgence as I not only lay down the law but also record my inner Talmudic process for arriving at it. For having determined that sex in advertising is an inevitable, and inevitably misused, by-product of the culture, I am left with the same nagging questions: In the twenty-first century, when is sex justifiably invoked? When is it gratuitous? When is it especially to the point? When is it simply too sexist and degrading to tolerate? When is it so sexy and compelling that nobody *cares* how degrading it is?

Obviously there are no pat answers. For one thing, one man's titillation is another man's travesty. But apart from individual subjectivity on questions of morality, there is the complicating matter of changing mores. Thresholds of acceptability and offensiveness shift with the culture, up and down, approximately like Rob Lowe's career. "The right thing to do" is a moving target that sometimes moves quite rapidly, such as right now. As recently as the midnineties most of what would be regarded as naked objectification had disappeared from advertising. Oh, there were still beautiful women (and men) showing up as meat puppets, but the blatancy that had characterized advertising sex objects had been substantially tamed. What the influence of feminist enlightenment did not fully achieves the terror of political correctness largely did. It was one thing to be called a chauvinist pig, another thing entirely to be regarded—under the construct of such feminist writers as Andrea Dworkin—as a rapist. Yes, take a deep breath and listen:

"Pornography is the orchestrated destruction of women's bodies and souls; rape, battery, incest, and prostitution animate it; dehumanization and sadism characterize it; it is war on women, serial assaults on dignity, identity, and human worth; it is tyranny. Each woman who has survived knows from the experience of her own life that pornography is captivity—the woman trapped in the picture used on the woman trapped wherever he's got her."

That's the radical-feminist scholar talking about the culture of pornography, advertising included. To Dworkin and her fellow travelers, media-image permissiveness is mistaken by men as sexual permission, and a Victoria's Secret commercial is therefore tantamount to sexual slavery. That may be a slight overstatement—OK, it's a preposterous, incendiary, and ultimately counterproductive overstatement—but it doesn't come from nothing.

Many critics, of course, believe advertising generally to be a malignant cancer in the culture. The writer and documentarian Jean Kilbourne, for example, writes that "all ads, in addition to selling products, sell us the idea that buying things can make us happy, that products can fulfill us and meet our deepest human needs. This leads to a never-ending cycle of consumption that ultimately disappoints us and that also endangers the environment. Yet another problem is that advertising so often objectifies women—and increasingly men as well—and fosters damaging stereotypes. Finally, some advertising sells products that are harmful and even addictive, often deliberately targeting children."

Kilbourne goes on to assert a direct connection between ubiquitous sexual imagery and violence, the sexual abuse of children, rape and sexual harassment, teenage pregnancy, and eating disorders. Also, I suppose, low SAT scores and the designated-hitter rule. True enough, though, her book *Deadly Persuasion* documents a terrifying array of overtly violent and dehumanizing advertising images of women, from submissive sexual positions to alcohol-enabled rape to assault at gunpoint. To see them is to gasp.

But no need to have the criticisms mouthed by sexual Chicken Littles. I myself have used my column as a bludgeon for years and years against those who trot out curvy women as eye candy (or, according to a 2001 study published in the brain-chemistry journal *Neuron,* pleasure-center-activating eye cocaine) for male viewers. Enough, I said, was enough.

I said it for years, actually, to no effect whatsoever. What finally caused advertisers to take heed was hardly my impassioned pleading, nor even the iron fist of political correctness. What made the Leading National Advertisers at last begin to see the error of their ways was a force far more powerful than the most inflammatory screeds of Dworkin, Catherine McKinnon, and Susan Faludi put together.

I refer, of course, to the Swedish Bikini Team.

The premise of this 1991 campaign by Hal Riney & Partners, San Francisco, for Old Milwaukee beer was ostensibly to send up the sexual preoccupations of the genre with the ultimate expression thereof: five Nordic goddesses in skimpy bikinis parachuting into scenes of male togetherness, cooing in (bad) Scandinavian accents, looking very blond and even more compliant. A spoof, the agency insisted—albeit one with tight close-ups of the fully endowed as a gift of fantasy for the not fully evolved.

The Swedish Bikini Team fiasco was, at a certain moment in history, the last straw. So brazen and infuriating was this display of pulchritude that female Stroh Brewing employees filed a class-action sexual harassment lawsuit. But unlike previous tempests over previous sexpots, this litigation didn't strike everybody as a silly, politicized stunt by a bunch of hypersensitive women's libbers. (It struck some people that way, of course. It struck George Will that way, but naturally it would, because it was class-action litigation against a corporation. If George Will went into the Hotel Sacher dining room, he'd demand torte reform.) This time around, the world took notice. Perhaps because Old Milwaukee's sales dropped precipitously, even the beer world took notice, as brewer after brewer publicly renounced the pinup-girl sensibility that had informed the industry at least since the Miss Rheingold pageants of the 1950s. Leading the suddenly enlightened was August Busch IV, the newly anointed vice president for marketing at Anheuser-Busch Co. Arguing that women were too important a customer base to be treated so basely, he declared sexist beer advertising to be an ugly artifact of the eighties and announced the debimbozation of his company's commercials. The Budweiser Doctrine was quickly embraced by other breweries. The video pinups all but disappeared. By 1995, Budweiser's central brand imagery consisted of three croaking frogs. A new age had dawned.

And lasted for exactly seven and a half years.

THE CLEAVAGE BOWL

"In the future, women [in Budweiser advertising] will have equal roles and be treated in an equal manner."
August Busch IV, 1991

"Read my lips: No new taxes."
George Herbert Walker Bush, 1988

Deobjectification had been a success three decades in the making. But then, in the life cycle of the cicada, everything changed back. Call it the reverse pendulum swing, call it recidivism, call it a surrender to biological and cultural reality—call it whatever you wish—but one day I turned on my TV and realized that the Budweiser Doctrine's brief, sensitive life was over.

The date was January 31, 1999. I tuned in to the Super Bowl and found it sponsored by a burlesque show, an astonishing cavalcade of spike heels and cleavage promoting everything from financial services to professional wrestling. There was the babe-o-licious former Miss USA Ali Landry sashaying through a gauntlet of drooling college boys to advertise Smokey Red Barbecue Doritos. There were the Victoria's Secret models shimmying (and also shimming) their perfectly spherical breasts an inch from the camera lens. There was an anonymous but tasty morsel of va-va-voomitude squeezed into a size-0 dress and pacing in front of a keyhole, on behalf of the Visa debit card. OK, sure, I might myself have, like, totally checked out the Visa woman, as she fulfilled at least fifteen of my top seventeen adolescent fantasies (sixteen if she could tie a sheepshank). But, still, women as playthings. Yuchhh. It was all so shockingly, unabashedly retro. And so damn confusing. But it was also, in its way, clarifying. The bizarre return to the culture's worst excesses helped me reconcile the basic human impulses documented at the beginning of this chapter with advertising's responsibility to uphold basic human dignity.

Now, advertising isn't quite a mirror image of society. And it isn't quite a snapshot—at least not the kind that you shoot and get back in twenty-four hours. Advertising (pay attention here to this apt and vivid metaphor, which I thought up myself) is more like the prints you process from a roll of film you shot a year ago and left baking in the glove compartment: accurate reflections of recent reality, somewhat distorted by heat and time. The Super Bowl filled an album. And, as I started to pay attention, I noticed similar excesses busting out everywhere. A contemporaneous print ad for a video game called "Virtual Pool II" showed a woman leaning over a pool table, exposing her bosom. "NICE RACK!" said the headline. A television commercial for Carl's Jr., the West Coast hamburger chain, showed a crowd of male office workers spying on a woman across the street, betting on whether the ultrajuicy burger would drip on her breasts. Then there was the magazine ad campaign featuring supermodel Rebecca Romijn-Stamos, who was photographed standing in the middle of the street, wearing a milk mustache, a bikini, and nothing else.

Sex in Milk Advertising. A new category, I believe.

Goodness gracious. These were the sort of outrages I'd been lashing out over for twenty years. I felt like a member of the World Health Organization, confident to the point of smugness about the eradication of smallpox, only to be witnessing a fresh outbreak. Which is to say: horrified, terrified, and embarrassed all at once. As if by reflex, immediately following the Cleavage Bowl, I unleashed a scathing postgame attack on the cynicism, the juvenile sensibilities, the moral backsliding that must have underwired it. Forgive me for quoting myself, but here's a brief sample of bile from the Affronted Critic:

> After three decades of gradually weaning itself from naked objectification, advertising has apparently decided that the benefit of crudely impressing men trumps the disadvantages of dishonoring women. It's as if Madison Avenue sneaked into the nation's psyche and absconded with thirty years of feminist awareness.

All right, so I was ticked. But I also was missing something. After all, if advertising truly reflects some sort of greater reality, the 1999 Super Bowl couldn't simply be pegged as unreconstructed sexism and reflexively denounced. Something else was clearly at work, and it's worth rummaging through some more overcooked snapshots—from advertising and elsewhere in the popular culture—to see what else they reveal about our twenty-first-century selves. (Warning: More history coming.)

For starters, you might credit Madonna. Just when the perniciousness of female objectification had been substantially understood and internalized by American society, along came the Boy Toy writhing in her underwear. This was very good for the recording industry. It was even better for the underwear industry. Frederick's of Hollywood had been in the black-bustier and lace-teddy business for decades, but then came Victoria's Secret to soften it and take it mainstream. And what about the Wonderbra? Twenty years after feminists burned their brassieres in protest, their heirs were burning their idealistic bridges and unapologetically displaying cleavage. Suddenly the guilt and ambivalence dissipated, and, under the rubric of empowerment, it was OK to be sexy. The push-up bra pushed up nothing if not self-esteem.

Then came the Spice Girls, trampy sex kittens whose "Girl Power" wasn't feminist self-actualization but the glorification of sexual leverage over men. Then feminist firebrand Bella Abzug died— of a broken heart, I'm guessing.

In the meantime, as we will further discuss in Chapter 6 of this unforgettable volume, the culture grew coarser by the minute, and advertising paralleled TV and movies—to paraphrase New York senator Daniel Patrick Moynihan—in defining outrageousness down. An industry that long had deliberately diluted, denatured, and dulled its output against the chance that somebody, somewhere might take offense now found itself intentionally inciting consumer outrage. It was a cynical bet: inflame the many to impress the few. Calvin Klein used sex to create outrage, which, in turn, was used to create buzz. A hundred advertisers followed.

Add to that new calculus the Ally McBeal/Bridget Jones Effect, a postfeminist license for women to feel incomplete without a man and to attract one by all means necessary. Is it any wonder, with the convergence of all of these forces, that we should have come to the end of the American Century in such a sexually aggressive state of mind, to the point that Doritos and Visa and a host of other advertisers suddenly felt emboldened to risk charges of neosexism and dabble in pinup marketing?

The "Ad Review" rebuke felt satisfying, but everything that I ever learned I learned from advertising, and in that very same week

I—as a collector of Kodak moments—blundered upon yet another revealing snapshot. This photo-artifact came not from Super Bowl 1999 but from a poster, in Grand Central Station, for Maidenform. It featured a beautiful brunette pictured from the waist up in nothing but a bra. "Inner beauty," the headline read, "only goes so far."

Oh, mercy. The lady was stunning, but not as stunning as the copy. Nobody is ever surprised when advertising evinces a nearly religious dedication to the superficial. What is astonishing is to see that mentality put forth as a brand benefit. Inner beauty *insufficient?* Nobody in the ad industry utters such things aloud, because, for one thing, it is sacrilege. You just don't say something like that. It's like suddenly reversing direction and telling your kid, "Oh, what the hell. Talk to strangers." No, what our parents taught us is that physical beauty is only skin deep and true worth resides in the soul. This universal article of faith stuck because it's righteous. It's democratic. It makes moral sense.

The only problem is, as Maidenform has observed, it simply isn't true. Niceness may count, but it doesn't turn heads. This may explain why—as contented as we may be with our inner selves and as distrustful as we may be about the beauty myth—most of us spend a portion of every day working on the exterior.

Now maybe this epiphany of mine doesn't turn your moral world upside down. Maybe it's, like, "Duh." But take the argument further. If people respond to other people simply because they are beautiful, what could be wrong, no matter what you're selling, with trotting out the most beautiful people you can find? Doritos and the bodacious, curvaceous Landry, to pick one extreme example. If it's just plain human to stare at impossibly attractive other humans, how can engineering that response be morally wrong, much less inhibited by niceties of social reform? Sex appeal is just too appealing, and if a bra ad is questioning all that is sacred, that means the metaconsciousness is questioning the same thing. Maidenform stated the premise. The Super Bowl offered the proof. The ensuing years of the Fox network fare have further rubbed our noses in it: society is clearly reevaluating, and the current consensus is that sexual correctness is a futile exercise in denial.

So what is God's appointed arbiter of advertising wisdom, what is a righteous man, what is a *father* to do?

IT AIN'T ROCKET SCIENCE

I have three daughters. Thinking of them, it has always been easy for me to respond to advertising cheesecake with my particular brand of antisexism boilerplate, because I wanted the vicious cycle to stop: a popular culture pandering to men's adolescent urges, leading women to trick themselves up correspondingly, leading to ever more degrading portrayals, leading to ever more female self-loathing, and so on, to oblivion. But, upon further reflection, what shall I do for my daughters—lie to them? What is served by lame pieties of an idealized physiognomy-blind world when the truth resides elsewhere? What good is it to scoff at their Victoria's Secret catalog as I glance at it, with great interest, over my teenager's shoulders? ("Wait, wait. Go back a page.")

OK now. I've posed a dozen versions of the same question. Comes now, finally, the answer—supplied not by me, the Apostle, but by an agency PR woman named Kathryn Woods. There need be no angst or conflict between inner and outer beauty in advertising, she told me, "As long as we can be whole people, I guess."

Whole people! And now I absolutely am, like, *duh*! Of course! People with an inner life *plus* a handsome exterior. It's a perfect standard. And, like Dorothy's revelation in liberated Oz, I guess I knew it all along—or at least since the 1973 "Dewar's Profile" of Sheila Ann T. Long, a rocket scientist engaged in mapping the world's electromagnetic field. A *drop-dead-gorgeous* twenty-eight-year-old rocket scientist, photographed in her Old Dominion University classroom in front of a chalkboard physics formula, wearing an expression that proclaimed, unequivocally, "Fly me."

This ad happened to be the subject of a fascinating college paper—a college paper of *mine*, itself eerily presaging a heroic career in advertising criticism. "They get you by your inherent scotch-drinker's snobbishness," young Robert Garfield wrote for English 115. "They get you by your desire to identify with extraordinary people. They get you by your balls." Well said, son. Dr. Long wasn't a Dewars profilee because she was a physicist; she was a Dewars profilee because she was a foxy physicist—which maybe isn't fair, but, I gotta tell you, it worked for me. (I'm happy to report that, despite numerous spelling errors, I got an A− on the paper. I'm equally pleased to report that Dr. Long's physics research for NASA two years later also yielded a paper, much like mine, only hers was titled "Derivation of Transformation Formulas Between Geocentric and Geodetic Coordinates for Nonzero Altitudes." It's available online, although I'm going to wait for the movie.)

Truth be told, I like looking at beautiful women. There have been times I've even been indecorous in this regard, allowing an appreciative glance to linger into something more of a leer. I'm not proud of this, exactly, but I'm not denying it either. Maybe I'm an innocent victim of the sexist culture. Maybe I'm an instinctive animal merely acting out my genetic imprint. Maybe I'm a billy goat. Maybe I'm just a pig. But, as my man Popeye so eloquently stated the proposition, "I yam what I yam and that's all that I yam." And so is most everybody else.

Is Sheila Ann T. Long, Ph.D., maybe a bit idealized? Of *course* she is idealized, but this is advertising we're talking about, not documentary. She's a real, honest-to-goodness whole person, and that meets the standard just fine.

Unfortunately, advertising generally is not only utterly uninterested in but also utterly incapable of portraying whole people. You can be sure that if advertising tried, the result would be a bare minimum of breathtakingly gorgeous real-life physicists and a whole lot of patronizing, unrealistic depictions of supermodel/philanthropists posing for *Vogue* in the morning and flying to Burundi in the afternoon to do hospice work. (Indeed, in the seventies and eighties, advertising created just such ridiculous Superwoman idealizations and still managed to be condescending. In one memorable example of the industry's distorted mirror, a TV spot for Prudential Bache showed a female law-firm dynamo being awarded a partnership. Then the senior partner took his beautiful and accomplished colleague aside and slipped her his broker's business card—because though she was a brilliant litigator with great legs, clearly she had no clue how to manage her newfound wealth without the help of the men.)

The answer, then, is not in plumbing The Many Facets of Everybody; it is in avoiding portrayals that are so objectifying, so limiting, so barren of character that they foreclose on any chance of imagining the depictee as a whole person, or of the target consumer imagining himself/herself as a whole person—as opposed to, say, a set of glands holding a remote control.

In other words, what we need to see is *potentially* whole people, maybe even breathtakingly beautiful potentially whole people. This would allow for a lot of hitherto frowned-upon babe-osity—the Maidenform model, for example, provided she is not presented as a hairdo and a pair of boobs, but a person, a whole person, exercising her God-given right to look better in a clingy knit. Applying this simple standard would still never justify depictions of women as sexual playthings. Rebecca Romijn-Stamos could still work—once she finishes her milk—but it would get that video game lady's breasts off the pool table. I could steal a guilty, admiring glance at a beautiful underwear model modeling underwear in an underwear catalog but still boycott the entertainment-for-men *Sports Illustrated* swimsuit issue.

Whether this is indeed moral backsliding or an adjustment to previous overcorrection I cannot say. What I can say is that values change, standards shift in ways that are often imperceptible absent the perspective of distance and time. That's why those snapshots come in so handy. They can't tell you whether the culture is advancing or regressing, but they certainly show what's changed since the last roll was processed.

Speaking for myself, as a critic, I bowed to my daughters' wishes and became less strident in attacking the beauty imperative. ("I don't read *Cosmo* to fulfill myself," my twenty-year-old explained. "I read it for the makeup samples.") On the other hand, society's values are one thing, and mine are quite another. And I'll still do my damnedest to see that Ali Landry—even if her Barbie doll body conceals an inner Mother Teresa—takes her Smokey Red Barbecue Doritos runway act strutting off of our TVs and out of our lives forever.

OGILVY WAS WRONG

This would be an extremely good time to remember Larry Walters.

On July 2, 1982, Walters piloted his experimental aeronautic vessel *Inspiration I* some sixteen thousand feet over Long Beach, California, and the Pacific Ocean. The thirty-two-year-old North Hollywood truck driver did so, damning the naysayers, in fulfillment of a lifelong dream to push the envelope of human achievement and soar into the wild blue yonder. His flight plan involved an eastward journey high above the Mojave Desert, but while this intrepid explorer had the Right Stuff, he had pretty much the wrong everything else. Unfavorable winds took Walters's craft in the opposite direction.

Commercial pilots were puzzled to see their landing paths into Los Angeles Airport encroached on by *Inspiration I*, which consisted of forty-two military-surplus helium weather balloons tethered by a fifty-foot cable to the command module.

The command module was a Sears aluminum lawn chair. Walters—shivering in the frigid air aloft—was reclining in it. Contrary to early reports from media eager to ridicule the man, he was not sucking on a beer. What he was doing was piloting his ass off.

Commander Walters had intended to hover only a thousand feet above ground but recognized well before liftoff that his calculations possibly could have lacked precision. He was equipped, therefore, for exactly this eventuality. On his lap he carried a Rapid Altitude Adjustment Device (i.e., a pellet gun), which, as the commander reached an altitude that made breathing difficult, he discharged into several of the balloons. He then gradually descended to a Long Beach neighborhood, where his aircraft was caught in high-tension power lines, blacking out portions of the city for twenty minutes.

And what prompted this modern-day Icarus to test the limits of folding backyard furniture? "It was something I had to do," he told the *Los Angeles Times*.

No, it wasn't. Risking death by lawn chair was not something Larry Walters had to do. But Larry, like millions of his fellow Americans, was stupid.

Stupidity, of course, comes in many forms: lack of judgment, like Larry; lack of intellect; lack of knowledge; lack of comprehension; lack of curiosity; lack of awareness; lack of common sense. It is not out of excess caution that perfume bottles include the warning "Do not pour over open flame;" it is out of grim experience. Likewise the consumer advisory on certain baby strollers: "WARNING: Remove child before folding." The annals of product-liability litigation are an ongoing testament to the mind-boggling stupidity of the public at large. And that stupidity manifests itself in so many other delicious ways.

I myself have sat in an Alexandria, Virginia, hotel conference room listening to a man named Erik Shrader assure people they can quickly earn $9 million per month with a multilevel marketing opportunity called the Omni Card, a credit card designed, he said, to work in reverse—paying *you* to spend money. For only a $60 membership fee and $25 per month, the select few gathered had the opportunity to recruit others for the sweetest deal going. Among those taking all this in was a woman named Claudia, who wore a purple print blouse, a purple vest, an "I Love Herbalife" button, and the world's last bouffant hairdo.

"I want to go for it!" she exclaimed shortly before producing her checkbook.

A few years later I stood in a Grenada Hills, California, parking lot and watched a woman shell out $5,000 for a business opportunity described, by a promoter named Holly thusly: "To buy into a business that's going to be good for the environment as well as for your pocketbook, per se, this is probably the least amount of money I've ever seen to get involved in a business to double your original investment after ten months and the second year make $20,000 to $30,000, if not more, depending on how aggressive you want to be."

The specific industry? Worm farming.

Of course, to understand this nation's vast reserve of dimness, and its corresponding vacuum of sophistication, you needn't sniff out get-rich-quick scams aimed at the most credulous. All you have to do is go to the strip mall and listen. At the video store recently I overheard the following conversation between two teenagers, who were ogling the lewd cover of some brain-dead Hollywood flick.

> **Teenager 1:** "Whoa! She's hot!"
> **Teenager 2:** "Yeah. You know what I noticed about TV? Even the ugliest girls on TV are hotter than the hottest chicks at our school."

Excellent insight, young fellow. My brother once stood outside of a Minneapolis movie theater, eavesdropping as the two people standing in front of him recognized each other from years back in high school:

Man: "So what are you doing?"

Woman: "I'm, like, a hairdresser. How about you?"

Man: "I'm with the FBI."

Woman: "Great! . . . What's that?"

Man: "Uh, the Federal Bureau of Investigation."

Woman: "Oh, yeah! Right! Great! . . . So that's like, what, a credit bureau?"

No reason to be surprised that this lady had reached the age of majority in the United States of America without becoming aware of the world's most famous police organization. Probably *Cosmopolitan* doesn't write much about the FBI.

Indeed, on the subject of reading matter, it's worth noting that the combined circulation of the *New Yorker* and the *Atlantic Monthly*—the two most widely distributed magazines of sophisticated journalism, criticism, fiction, and humor—is 1.45 million. This represents less than half of the combined circulation of the *National Enquirer* and *Soap Opera Digest*. Just to put that further in perspective, here is a little excerpt from an interview by *SOD*'s Suzanne Byrne with Tonya Lee Williams, who plays Dr. Olivia Winters on CBS's "The Young and the Restless."

Byrne: Do you think Liv is genuinely in love with Neil?

Williams: I think that she thinks she is. In Olivia's mind, there's something between them from way, way back. In reality, I don't know if there really is something there, or if she's just convinced herself that they're the most compatible couple. I'm not sure she's seeing Neil for who he is today. But Olivia believes that they are, and that's the most important thing.

Byrne: But it appears that Neil has his eye on Alex. How does Olivia feel about her new competitor?

Williams: Olivia completely doesn't like Alex. Alex represents everything that Olivia doesn't like in professional women. She's antagonistic and hard and—more importantly—she's seeing Olivia's ex-husband. But as much as Olivia doesn't like her now, I think she will just be completely insane and despise the woman completely when it comes out that Neil is harboring feelings for Alex, too.

Note to the stupid: Olivia, Neil, and Alex are pretend.

As for the *Enquirer*, in its first issue after the September 11, 2001, World Trade Center catastrophe, which killed three thousand people and fomented a global war, the headline was as follows: "Tom: I Know Who Got Nicole Pregnant." Furthermore, and finally, because I don't believe these words require embellishment: professional wrestling.

THE TARGET CONSUMER DOESN'T DRINK CHAI

It has become a commonplace to suggest that advertising insults people's intelligence, and that is sometimes true. More often, though, exactly the opposite is the case. Advertising gives more credit for brains, judgment, and sophistication than is reasonably due—no matter what your inherent sense of egalitarianism and respect for dead advertising legends may mislead you to believe. Yes, I refer to David Ogilvy, who is famous for observing, "The consumer isn't a moron. She is your wife."

Well, David, God rest your soul, but that's just not so. The consumer—the average consumer—isn't some ad guy's wife. She is Claudia, the Omni Card sucker. She is the young lady in the movie line. She is Holly the worm-wrangler, per se. Or, prototypically, she is Wanda, the wife of a forklift operator at a Piggly Wiggly in Chattanooga, Tennessee. She watches "Temptation Island." She has not read a newspaper since high school civics class. Her tidy home is stuffed with velour-covered furniture, and her walls are covered with bric-a-brac from the Bradford Exchange. The Footprints in the Sand "Precious Moments" collector plate is her favorite, although she also loves the Elegant Dancers plate, featuring twin dolphins frolicking in the ocean blue.

And she frequently hasn't the slightest clue as to what you're talking about. That bears repeating: *not the slightest clue as to what you're talking about.*

That's a big problem in advertising. Creatives are all the time writing ads for one another or for themselves. Quite frequently they write ads for one another or themselves and harvest trophies for their efforts. The clients, however, harvest no such trophies. What the clients harvest is failure, because somehow in the euphoria of the creative process they fall into the thrall of the Clever Ones who typically misunderstand what the target audience—or the world at large—is really like. Or, put another way: they haven't the vaguest idea about what the prospect doesn't have the vaguest idea about.

It's not an IQ issue, necessarily (although sometimes the smartest advertising is smart because it understands the fat part of the bell curve). Mainly it's a sensibilities issue. For instance, as I once observed in my column, you can search all the reception areas of all the agencies in all the cities, and you will never, *ever* see a big sofa with maple-trimmed arms and brown tweed fabric beneath some sort of pewter wall hanging of an eagle clenching arrows in its talons.

Why is this? Well, first, as anyone dressed all in black will tell you, these things are ugly—objectively ugly, according to science and nature and the immutable laws of the cosmos. Highly educated, urban, coastal, and generally well-to-do ad people simply are not an

Early American crowd. They are *so* not an Early American crowd, in fact, so confident in their rarefied tastes and smug in their aesthetic superiority, that they are scarcely *aware* of an Early American crowd.

But there's the problem: most of the country *is* an Early American crowd. There is a whole big population out there, and it isn't reading *Architectural Digest*, watching foreign films, and sipping chai. It is reading *Parade*, watching Stallone, and swilling Bud. Nixon called this population the Silent Majority, and that was one thing he wasn't delusional about. The Silent Majority is real. It's what they now call Middle America, although by no means do you have to go to the middle of America to find it. Yes, it's well represented in Iowa, the sensible shoes capital of the world, but it's also in Pasadena and Miami and Queens, New York. It eats Kraft macaroni and cheese, it reads romance novels, and it smokes. It doesn't know who Robert Mapplethorpe was, it doesn't understand that Early American sofas (or, worse yet, chrome-trimmed "contemporary" sectionals) are mockeries of God's plan, but it sure has most of the money for buying the products that advertising people stupidly persist in advertising hiply to their own elitist selves.

SEE DICK. SEE DICK RUN.
SEE DICK FALL ON HIS SMIRKING FACE.

To cite one tiny example: a Philips spot for the flat TV, filled with funky, edgy, lower-Manhattan young dot-commers. Very cool—except the people who buy $4,000 TVs are mainly sitting in Barcaloungers watching "Cops" or "Touched by an Angel" or NASCAR. Just curious here: if your target audience isn't ultrahip young lower-Manhattan dot-commers, why would you populate your ad with characters whom your audience not only can't relate to but probably despises to the core of their beings?

I could cite dozens of examples of ads that fail before they ever leave the agency, solely because they are over the heads—or, more precisely, out of sync with the lives—of their principal targets. Instead, though, let's talk about only two campaigns, which happen to be the work of the same advertiser. One is a brilliant example of how witty, entertaining TV commercials can forge a relationship with the target consumers because it utterly understands their preoccupations, their joys, their prejudices, their idiosyncrasies—in short, their lifestyles. The other is the quintessential example of how witty, entertaining TV commercials can devastate one of the world's leading brands.

That brand is Miller Lite. You know the basic story; it's one for the marketing annals, a landmark triumph built—beginning, nationally, in 1975—on the convergence of simple demographics and simple carbohydrates.

Just as the guts of beer-swilling baby boomers started to expand, along came Lite's alluring promise of "Tastes great! Less filling!" It happened that Lite didn't taste great; it was watery. And "less filling" was just a euphemism for less alcohol. But it was a compromise lumpy boomers could live with. Through years of funny ads from the old Backer & Spielvogel agency featuring self-deprecating ex-jocks debating the primacy of the dual brand benefits, Lite became America's number-two beer, destined it seemed even to challenge Budweiser.

Lite, alas, never quite got there (although Bud Light, in 2001, would). In 1990, sales peaked at 19.9 million barrels, for a 10.3 percent share. That's when Miller and its new agency, Leo Burnett USA, determined that ex-jocks were no longer relevant. They repositioned the brand not as the first choice in light beers but as the first choice in beers, period, for the fun-loving young generation. Everybeer, you might say, for everyman.

No such luck. A succession of campaigns took spectacular belly flops, including "It's It and That's That," "Can Your Beer Do This?" and "Life Is Good." By 1997, shipments were down to 15.9 million barrels per year and market share of only 8.5 percent—a slide partly attributable to the demographic fact that boomers are long past prime guzzling age. But it's also true that younger drinkers brought up in a hard-body culture have come to prefer light beers themselves. And the one they prefer is Bud Light.

Maybe that's because Anheuser-Busch single-mindedly supported its brand, while Miller depleted resources chasing transitory niches, such as Southpaw Light, a fake "boutique" beer, and the preposterous, disastrous Miller Clear. But there was also the advertising itself. Pursuing much the same creative strategy as Burnett, DDB Worldwide came up with catch phrase after memorable Bud Light catch phrase. Yes, they did. And people loved it, man. Lite, meanwhile, faded into the distance. Losing ground and losing hope, Miller turned to Fallon McElligott, Minneapolis, one of the world's most creative shops. Fallon responded not by trying to rediscover the essence of the Lite brand or by finding something relevant to say to the consumer but by simply trying to imbue Lite with more personality than the competition. The result was "Dick," an ad campaign about the ad-making process:

"This is Dick," the introductory TV spot began. "Dick is a creative superstar, and the man behind the advertising you are about to witness. We gave Dick a six-pack of Miller Lite and some money and asked him to come up with a commercial for Miller Lite . . ."

Only "he" didn't. He came up with some inside jokes, some amusingly dated graphics, and several self-indulgent commercials about Dick.

One of the first depicted a lone man walking through a wheat field in a hat, bow tie, and coat. Only when he emerged from the waves of grain was it revealed that he was wearing nothing else from the waist down—except the Lite logo. In another from the first pool, a magician vanished some small, furry rodents—the fur from which materialized beneath the underarms of his curvaceous assistant.

The creators of these goofy non sequiturs were essentially knocking off their similarly goofy non sequiturs from back when they were in the employ of DDB Paradiset, the Stockholm agency that had wowed Cannes with a high-attitude, high-irony, high-pop-culture-referential campaign for Diesel jeans. And the strategy—such as it was—was identical: to cultivate young beer drinkers by lampooning the notion of advertising itself and ostentatiously eschewing dubious positive statements about the brand. They sought to command your attention to announce how subversively absurd they were.

The arch, oddball spots were defiantly postmodern, all right, and there were those who were taken in. They mistook the campaign's world-weary drollness for clarity of thought, believing Dick—who just happened to share a nickname with a famous sex organ—to be the apotheosis of antiadvertising. But he wasn't that at all. He was just advertising, a particularly smug, masturbatory sort of advertising.

Now wasn't that just grand? For forty years, the gullible and paranoid have believed that art directors manipulate their consumer libidos by hiding penises in their ads and, lo and behold, colloquially speaking, courtesy of Fallon McElligott, there one was. O, those wicked boys and their offbeat ostentation! O, the knowing winks at the High Camp of self-reference! O, the genius of flattering GeneratioNext with how hip and sophisticated and mediawise they are!

O, the stupidity.

If this campaign had been targeted at thirty-year-old, college-educated, Swedish art directors obsessed with American pop culture, it would have been dead-on perfect. But it wasn't—a failure immediately evident to beer wholesalers, retailers, advertising critics, and everyone except the agency itself. How I love to read and reread excerpts from an article by Fallon executive Mark Goldstein published in 1998 in a trade magazine called *Integrated Marketing & Promotion*: "We have a great sense of what the consumer will allow a brand to be. The best example is probably the most controversial, Miller Lite. *Advertising Age*, writing from its usual perch in the 1950s, trashed the Miller Lite campaign brutally. . . . In truth, we knew before the first Miller spot ever aired that we had a winner. The consumer told us. Account planning paved the way for a campaign that—while confusing to 40-year-olds—was a laser beam to twenty-one- to twenty-five-year-old men."

Well, speaking from my perch in the twenty-first century, I think I can safely conclude that Dick wasn't a laser at all. He was more like a blunderbuss, yielding some noise and smoke and little else. Turned out, twenty-one- to twenty-five-year-old men weren't especially captivated by the campaign. Mainly they were bewildered. And older drinkers—the core of the Miller Lite franchise—were largely alienated. As in, totally pissed off. Oh, sure, there were some who did, indeed, appreciate the hipness and attitude of the campaign, but most did not, and beer advertising is a most-of-them proposition—including a large number of total slobs. These are not rarefied tastes we're talking about. They are better served with substance, or even fantasy, not faux nihilism.

By the time Miller finally played Lorena Bobbitt to Fallon's "Dick"—despite several hundred millions of dollars of ad spending and deep wholesaler discounting to artificially pump up volume—market share for Lite had plummeted still *further* to 7.9 percent. "Dick" failed not because it was unclever. Truthfully, it was quite clever and at various points, to the discerning eye, substantially brilliant. (A late spot showed a goofy-looking guy in his underwear, in the kitchen, for no apparent reason doing a sixties-era dance in front of his Lite bottle. A close-up of the bottle cap finally revealed what he was up to. The cap said, "Twist to open." Take my word for it; it was funnier and more charming than it sounds and finally—unlike most previous spots from the campaign—actually about drinking beer.) The problem was the obvious paucity of discerning eyes in the target audience. In other words, the campaign tanked because it was too clever by half.

DUCT TAPE AND DARRYL

Oddly, at about the time the advertiser was ready to pull the plug on "Dick," Miller Brewing Co. came up with the perfect Miller Lite campaign. It was funny, targeted, relevant, dead center on the demographic. There was only one problem. The perfect Lite campaign— at least what should have been the Lite campaign—was launched on behalf of Miller High Life.

High Life was a venerable old brand that had been left for dead in 1989 by the same astute marketing minds that mismanaged Lite into its sorry state. "The champagne of beers" had become a fringe player, barely advertised and languishing pitifully in the popular-price segment. How a beer that once outsold Budweiser could have been so neglected is another one for the annals, but we'll put that aside. In 1998 Miller decided to breathe some high life into its moribund, ex-marquee product with a campaign from Wieden & Kennedy, Portland, Oregon—a campaign that demonstrated that someone at the brewery, at long last, was using his head. The series of fifteen-second spots proved, among other things, that cleverness doesn't mean being regarded as clever by those who drink imports and chichi microbrews in a variety of earth tones but by those reasonably expected to purchase your product. You know: guys named Darryl.

Darryl is Wanda's husband. He lives in Chattanooga. He struggled in high school. He's a forklift operator/management trainee over to the Piggly Wiggly. He loves God, country, Mom, Dad, his stepmom and stepdad, Jeff Gordon, and the "Jerry Springer Show" out-take video. Darryl drinks 80 percent of the beer in the continental United States, and—whether he is thirty-three and slowing down or eighteen and just getting into his guzzling prime—he has no interest in postmodern absurdity. He's not stupid, but he's not sophisticated either. And just because he's young and media immersed and wears an earring doesn't mean he's particularly media savvy. He doesn't get irony. All he gets is thirsty.

Breweries have known about Darryl for years, of course. That's why beer advertising historically played into his perceived sensibili-ties: unquestioning patriotism, pride in a hard day's work, nice-looking babes squeezed into their clothing like an insurance doctor in a latex glove. But now the trend is to make Darryl laugh. Bud Light has been doing a pretty good job of it for a decade, mainly by showing the efforts of a bunch of henpecked guys to elude their wives on week-ends and sock down brewskies while watching sports on TV. Bud has frogs and lizards and guys saying "Whasssuuuup?" As for Lite, well, as we know, it has the calorie-conscious Ph.D.-in-semiotics market just about locked up. So how could High Life be funny in a way dif-ferentiating itself from how Bud products are funny, without alien-ating Darryl and his gimme-cap-wearing friends? The answer was inspired: a series of spots poking gentle, reverent fun at all the val-ues Darryl holds dear.

One—the showcase one—showed a guy on his roof, doing a major repair job entirely with duct tape.

"The High Life Man knows that if the pharaohs had duct tape, the Sphinx would still have a nose," the gravelly, deep-voiced, archly plain-speaking narrator said. "We salute you, duct tape. You help a man get to Miller Time."

Another spot showed a guy snacking on doughnuts while work-ing on his car: "The powdered sugar on this doughnut," the voice-over asserted, "puts a semiprotective barrier between your fingerprint and your nutrition." Yet another showed a guy struggling to back his boat trailer into the driveway, to the chagrin of a neighbor and the profound disappointment of the narrator: "Time was a man knew how to command his own vehicle. Just how far are we willing to fall? Better reacquaint yourself with the High Life, soldier, before someone tries to take away your Miller Time."

The campaign, in its fourth year at this writing, won Darryl's attention not by being offbeat but by hilariously capturing the rhythms of his life. The humor, about the peccadilloes of the demographic, paid warmhearted tribute to the consumer, not to the creative team. It honored Darryl by teasing him but in no way speaking down to him. Far from the smug condescension of Dick, this campaign respected who Darryl is.

And, unlike anything else Miller did for an entire decade, it worked. High Life gained volume—about a 4 percent increase—but more important, stopped what had been a precipitous drop in market share. The erstwhile champagne of beers had slid to a pathetic 2.6 percent share of domestic beer sales. At this writing High Life fluctuates between 2.8 percent and 2.9 percent—still pretty pathetic but clearly moving in the right direction. Moreover, it is doing so, once again, at premium prices.

Now look here: in no way am I suggesting that the people who create advertising campaigns should go for the lowest common denominator. That would be insane. TV advertising did so for decades and continues to pay the price today in consumer disaffection, suspicion, even hostility toward commercial messages. The notion of advertising's insulting people's intelligence became a commonplace because, for the first thirty years of their existence, commercials *did* routinely insult people's intelligence—in addition to bludgeoning them into submission with brand messages and phony Unique Selling Propositions wielded like truncheons. This relentless battering may have seemed useful and efficient in its day, when the old Ted Bates agency, for instance, would spare no irritant or exaggeration to communicate some dubious brand distinction. Nobody ever questioned the utility of "humorous" characters like Josephine the Plumber (Comet Cleanser) or Madge the Manicurist (Palmolive Liquid) in browbeating viewers with decreasingly bearable, allegedly comic iterations of the same selling point. Nobody seemed to notice that assaulting the viewer took its toll, even as advertisers found themselves requiring ever greater media tonnage to achieve the same effect. It was like producing electricity by burning cheap, sulfur-laden soft coal. In the short term, that seemed like a bargain, but the long-term cost of cleaning sulfur dioxide from the atmosphere dramatically increased the cost of business for everybody. Advertising that polluted the airwaves had a parallel effect—an effect that became especially apparent when the three-network universe disappeared. Suddenly consumers found themselves wired for cable, armed with a remote control, and capable of obliterating any commercial they didn't find instantly engaging. Which, gleefully, consumers did. The amount of media weight, measured in Gross Ratings Points, required to achieve the same effect in, say, unaided recall, soared. Some bargain.

So of course—in a hundred-channel, TiVo environment—advertising must amuse, seduce, entertain, or otherwise enthrall viewers as it goes about its business. The days of bluster and bloviation are long gone, and good riddance. But what amuses, seduces, entertains, and enthralls me, or you, or a conference room full of agency people with Soho addresses, is apt to be very different from what amuses, seduces, entertains, and enthralls Wanda and Darryl and the exactly 50 percent of the consuming public who are stupider than average. Bear in mind that you must impress the target audience even if, in all likelihood, the target audience doesn't impress you. I've spent a lot of time invoking Shakespeare in this book, and I'm going to do it again, because Shakespeare internalized this concept like no other.

Yes, his plays were poetically rendered masterpieces with breathtaking understanding of human psychology, but, for the fat part of the Elizabethan bell curve filling the seats in the Globe Theater, the plays were also perfectly accessible soap opera, with convoluted plots, sinister characters, mistaken identities, sex, and savagery galore. When, in *Hamlet*, Polonius gave Laertes his marching orders ("Neither a borrower, nor a lender be. . . . to thine own self be true," etc.), he might easily have added, "Know thine audience." On that thought, I leave you with one more item from the annals of Folding Aluminum Chair Genius:

> BUXTON, N.C., Aug. 9, 1997 (AP)—A man died on a beach when an 8-foot-deep hole he had dug into the sand caved in as he sat inside it. Beachgoers said Daniel _____, 21, dug the hole for fun, or protection from the wind, and had been sitting in a beach chair at the bottom Thursday afternoon when it collapsed, burying him beneath 5 feet of sand. People on the beach on the Outer Banks used their hands and shovels, trying to claw their way to _____, a resident of Woodbridge, Va., but could not reach him. It took rescue workers using heavy equipment almost an hour to free him while about 200 people looked on. _____ was pronounced dead at a hospital.

DOA, the poor dope, like the Lite campaign and a thousand others that collapse in on themselves for want of even a rudimentary strategic infrastructure to shore up their walls of sand.

CHAPTER **6**

BE MY GUEST

I know, I know. Everybody has problems, but I have had just the *worst* ten years, advertising-wise. You won't believe some of the things that have happened to me.

First, in 1993, I had this great punditry gig with CBS as a frequent guest on morning television, where I was expected to be refreshingly acerbic about TV commercials. But one day I got caught in the Green Room being refreshingly acerbic about CBS's pitiful morning-television audience and got my pundit ass summarily fired. Then, in 1996, I was a guest in scenic St. Croix, U.S. Virgin Islands, brought in to give a speech to some advertising group, and got slightly kidnapped by some guys with stockings over their heads and guns and plans—according to the FBI—to eventually shoot me to death. I managed to escape, which was cool, plus the speech went well, but the whole episode sent me spiraling into a debilitating depression, which sucked.

Then, this other time . . . well, do you know Leo Burnett? Leo Burnett Co. Huge Chicago-based agency. "Reach for the stars." Tony the Tiger. Mr. Clean. Pillsbury Doughboy. Yeah, well, as God is my witness, this happened: Leo Burnett barged into my family room, strictly uninvited, and incited my children to hate me. He told 'em to crank their video games till the adults couldn't stand it. Burped in my face and advised the kids, most graphically, that life is for spitting on.

It was a Burnett commercial for Nintendo, from 1994, and the idea was to win the fealty of teenage boys by cultivating their predisposition to defy authority. No surprise there; a hundred advertisers, from Bubble Tape to 7UP to you-name-it, have depicted adults as clueless objects of ridicule, to be dismissed if not actually despised. But this was beyond the pale. Opening with a too-smiley, too-coiffed Mom expressing her dream to have a doctor in the family, the ad announced its intentions with a close-up of her teenager's response: a loud, close-up belch. Then, to the dulcet croonings and empathetic sentiments of, naturally, the Butthole Surfers ("We wanna be free. We wanna do what we wanna do. We wanna have a good time, and that's exactly what we're gonna do."), came the suggestion to crank up Mortal Kombat, or whatever, to full volume, because it freaks out the grown-ups. "Be heard," went the slogan. "Play it loud."

Yes, the sensitive marketing professionals at Nintendo and Burnett, having divined a certain restlessness, frustration, and inchoate hostility among adolescents and preteens, were trying to reach these young people in sympathetic terms. Nintendo, they suggested, was a perfect badge of sullen militancy. At one point in the spot, the kid snarfles up a wad of phlegm and spits it at the audience, with the accompanying instruction to "Hock a loogie at life."

What a charming idea. Tell kids that adults don't listen to them. Pour gasoline on the fire of teenage anger. Encourage them to be rude. Ridicule authority figures, parental and otherwise, as decorum-obsessed dweebs. Assist young people in their often perilous search for identity by suggesting they embrace the most garish kind of self-centered nihilism. By all means, exploit the pain and confusion of adolescence by admonishing our children that life is to be defiled. What greater service can an advertiser perform, against the backdrop of teen suicide, for example, than to trumpet the meaninglessness of human existence?

Bravo, you cynical bastards. And congratulations to you, Leo, for having the wisdom to be dead during all of this. For wasn't it you who wrote, upon your retirement, the following? "When you show the slightest sign of crudeness, inappropriateness or smart-aleckness—and you lose that subtle sense of the fitness of things. . . . That, boys and girls, is when I shall insist you take my name off the door . . . even if I have to materialize long enough some night to rub it out myself—on every one of your floors."

Well, sir, now I understand the Publicis deal. I thought it was about money. But maybe it's about the founder's shame from beyond.

In any event, the mischief hardly ends there. Shortly before Burnett's home invasion crime, Roy Rogers Restaurants had also stormed our house, telling death jokes, one after another. A couple of them—like the one about the fellow being eaten by a wild animal—were kind of funny, but overall just too morbid for words. (Generally speaking, in the fast-food category, sudden death is not considered an enticement.) Then, in the middle of a Sunday football game I was watching with my little girls, a man and woman materialized five feet in front of my recliner, pawing each other like dancing bears. *Hey, kids, check out the guy burrowing his head in the lady's cleavage!* Then, of course, there is Benetton, which, under the flimsiest pretext of sociopolitical commentary, has promulgated a series of shocking images calculated to inflame, provoke, and horrify millions of people who are in no way prospective customers for $40 T-shirts. A photo of a priest kissing a nun was a blasphemy to Catholics worldwide. And images of a dead soldier's bloody clothing, a dead AIDS victim, boat people clinging to a ship's netting like so many vermin, and Ronald Reagan retouched to appear to have Kaposi's sarcoma have been pokes in the eye for millions more who don't wish to get their political commentary from a sportswear retailer.

And on it goes. And on, and on, and on.

The Nintendo episode, because it so perversely preys on children and so brazenly ignores their welfare, is probably the vilest advertising obscenity I've ever encountered. It is by no means, however, uniquely repulsive. In this chapter you will find too many stomach-turning examples of shockvertising—examples so extreme you may think I'm making them up, which, unfortunately, I am not. Some are violent. Some are graphically scatological. Some are overtly sexual. Some are mean. What they all have in common, though, is the malignant inconsideration for the audiences that see them, *never having asked to see them*, thus becoming random victims of advertising assault.

Let's go back, for example, to 1996 and a McCabe & Co., New York, TV spot called "Big Buford." It was for a southeastern chain of burger joints called Rallys, and its target audience, we can only hope, was young men. The commercial opened at a traffic light, where two blue-collar dudes in a pickup truck watched enviously as a convertible pulled up next to them with a guy driving and two beautiful babes aboard.

"What's he got that I ain't got?" the pickup driver asked his friend.

"Oh," the friend replied matter-of-factly, "he's probably got a Big Buford."

The driver stared downward in astonishment: "Look at the size of that thing!"

"Yeah," the friend continued, "it's a third of a pound. Two beef patties, double cheese, lettuce, tomato, pickles, onions. The works." This, to the picture of the women in the car eating their burgers in a sexually suggestive way. Lots of advertising is fallacious. This was fellatious—right up to the mayonnaise smeared around their lips.

"You like 'em big, huh?" the leering driver asked one of the women.

"It's not the size," she answered coyly. "It's the taste, stupid."

No, it's the lack of taste. The creator of this campaign, Ed McCabe (legendary Creative Revolutionary and member of the Copywriters Hall of Fame), somehow forgot that television is a mass medium. No doubt the target audience laughed their adolescent asses off. But the spot scandalized so many non-big-penis-joke aficionados that it was promptly pulled from the air, just as shortly thereafter the Rallys account was pulled from the agency. Even before that, though, the spot was raked over the coals in "Ad Review" (0 stars), prompting the maestro to write a letter to *Advertising Age* questioning whether my harsh appraisal reflected some insecurity I might have had about my own, personal . . . uh . . . Buford. Ed McCabe's missive was so childish, so demeaning, and so basically beneath contempt that my editors simply took it and published it in our magazine.

That was a nice chapter in my career. And about the last in Ed's.

DEATH, MENTAL ILLNESS, AND OTHER HILARIOUS MATERIAL

It is often said of the smart aleck, "A thought never crossed his mind that didn't also pass his lips." This refers to the incautiousness and pathological lack of self-control that makes even the cleverest of wags a threat to himself and others when an intemperate remark backfires. It happened to Ed, and it happened in 1990 to Chiat/Day.

The commercial in question was for the Reebok Pump, a sneaker with an inflatable air bladder in the tongue, supposedly offering a snugger fit. To illustrate the product attribute, Chiat/Day filmed a grainy, docu-style vignette depicting a bungee adventurer attempting a daring bridge jump in Washington state's Deception Pass. His bungee, however, was tethered to his non-Reebok sneaker. In the final shot, viewers saw nothing but the shoe and the bungee cord dangling from the bridge.

It was meant to be black humor and no doubt was taken as such by much of the target audience. The realism was so convincing, however, and the tragic denouement of violent death on the rocks of Puget Sound so apparent, that viewers were horrified. Reebok was forced to pull the spot in the uproar.

The same happened in 1994 to the New York agency DeVito/ Verdi. In an attempt to attract attention to the beleaguered clothier Britches Great Outdoors, the agency created one of the most wickedly funny cinema verité commercials ever filmed. Also shot in black and white, it depicted six grim pallbearers emerging from an old church with a casket. With somber deliberation, they shouldered their burden toward a waiting hearse, slid in the coffin, and slammed the door. "You're going to be wearing a suit for a long time," said the voice-over. "Dress comfortably . . . while you can."

A great gag and not an uncompelling argument. The problem was that the whole thing was built on the stark, sobering, very verité first twenty-five seconds, into which each viewer couldn't help injecting his own experience with funerals and death. By the time the punch line came along—the first time you realized there would *be* a punch line—it was impossible not to imagine a friend or loved one in the coffin. Maybe some in the audience still laughed, but plenty no doubt felt betrayed and insulted by the grim twist. And no matter how amused Britches' youthful target audience and other thick-skinned viewers may have been, there is no excuse for toying with the emotions of everybody else. That spot was quickly yanked, too, as well it should have been.

The lesson: just because you think of something clever to say doesn't mean you necessarily should say it.

The same mistake was made in 1994 by Nike in a football-season campaign starring Dennis Hopper. Synthesizing his deranged roles in *Blue Velvet*, *Hoosiers*, and *Apocalypse Now*, Hopper played the ultimate rabid football fan. The story line was ambiguous, but he either was an ex-NFL referee drummed out of the officials' corps because of bizarre on-the-field behavior, or he simply imagined himself to be an NFL ref. Either way, he dressed in zebra stripes and a ratty trench coat, the picture of dishevelment, wandering from stadium to stadium, ranting semicoherently about the magnificence of such NFL stars (and Nike endorsers) as Buffalo Bill Bruce Smith, Dallas Cowboy Troy Aikman, and Detroit Lion Barry Sanders. In one spot he has sneaked into the Bills' locker room and exulted about Smith's ferocity while sniffing the player's football shoe. "He does bad things, man. *Bad* things." In another spot he claimed to see Barry Sanders's backfield-escape moves in his sleep, whereupon he stepped toward the camera and added, "And I don't sleep that much."

Let us leave aside for the moment the question of what all that had to do with selling shoes. Let's give Nike the benefit of the doubt and say the dark humor and over-the-top characterization of the Hopper spots serve to enhance, and advance, the company's edgy brand image. Speaking for myself, I'm a huge Dennis Hopper fan, and the spots made me laugh out loud, especially the insomnia line. But uncomfortable laughter it was. Guilty laughter, actually, because Referee Dennis was not an eccentric. He was a loon, a troubled, sick man—a paranoid schizophrenic, by all appearances—and he shouldn't have been shoe sniffing in TV commercials. Why? Because to large numbers of the viewing audience there is nothing funny about a persuasive depiction of a man losing his grip on reality. Someone who has suffered the unspeakable ongoing tragedy of schizophrenia, as a patient or a loved one, would have every reason to watch the Hopper spots and shudder.

Shoe advertising has no right to make the viewer shudder.

No advertising has the right to make the viewer shudder. Let me ask you a question: would you ever knock on a stranger's door and, upon being permitted to enter—wait, let me plumb the darkest recesses of my imagination—OK, how about . . . *produce a kitchen blender and use it to puree a human brain*? Is there a single person reading this who would do such a thing? No, because it would be sick. It wouldn't be black humor. It wouldn't be deliciously subversive. It wouldn't be guerilla marketing. It would be an affront, indecent and unforgivable.

Brought to you by Hasbro. Yes, the nice folks behind G. I. Joe, Mr. Potato Head, and the Easy Bake toy oven in 2001 created a commercial about pulverizing a human brain (or, at least, a perfect facsimile) in a blender. The product being advertised was Nemesis Factor, an electronic puzzle targeted at players ten to adult. That's ten years old. That's fourth grade. That's still curling up with a special blankie at night. A second spot, out of an abundance of sensitivity, did not depict a brain being chopped in a blender. It depicted a brain being submerged into a deep fryer.

Obviously, these spots from Jordan, McGrath Case, & Partners, New York, were targeted not at the ten-year-old portion of the prospective marketplace but at the adolescent-to-young-adult-male portion—a demographic notably amused by gross-outs. But, once and for all, *the target is irrelevant*. Advertising is a shotgun, not a rifle. When it fires, anything near the target is caught in the spray. Is that so difficult to grasp? If some dim all-in-black is too self-involved to internalize that axiom and exhibit some modicum of human decency, you would think at least the Hasbro client would get it. This is a company that markets both Play-Doh and Dungeons & Dragons. If ever there were a business that should realize that different audiences have different sensibilities, it is this one. They more than most should understand, for example, that some fifteen-year-old boy in the family might think the blender stunt was the single coolest thing he'd ever seen. But that Mom will be crying and throwing up, Dad will be calling the police, and little Sis will have night terrors for the rest of her life.

At long last, please, internalize this critical point: commercials are not programming. Nobody has chosen to see one. TV spots simply appear, and in exchange for viewer indulgence advertisers owe a measure of restraint and respect for the sensitivities of everyone in the room. Not just the target. Everyone. That is advertisers' unspoken compact with viewers. That has always been the compact. And this advertiser Hasbroken it.

F YOU, CK

Hasbro never made it to Cannes, although there is no doubt in my mind that it would have, had the spots not been pulled immediately after my column appeared. In general, Cannes is most hospitable to even the most gruesome imagery—partly for all the reasons cited so far and partly because the spots are screened there in gigantic auditoriums, as if they were avant-garde cinema. But, as we have long since established, they are not avant-garde cinema. They are just commercials, sales messages that should be designed not to impress a theater full of similarly misguided souls but to show up in real people's family rooms far from the French Riviera where actual consumers watch them during *Wheel of Fortune* while they're trying to wolf down dinner.

The actual purpose of advertising and its actual effects do not seem to be major considerations on the festival circuit. In 1998, a ninety-second documentary-style spot from TBWA GGT Simons Palmer screened at Cannes. The action took place in the kitchen of a fancy restaurant, focusing on a sous chef adding his personal touch to the dishes. He took a swig of brandy, for instance, and gargled it before adding it to the flambé. He picked his nose and rolled the snot up for placement atop an hors d'oeuvre. He took a steak and wiped it on the inside of a filthy toilet. All of this in close-up to increasingly pained groans from the crowd. The product: PlayStation. The message: Stay home.

It won a gold Lion.

Or take the 1996 spot from Young & Rubicam, Zurich, for a brand called Hakle. It showed a man at the beach, back to the camera, looking toward the ocean. He wore tight striped swim trunks, which dominated the foreground of the shot. As the spot opened, a fly buzzed into the picture, near his swimsuit, and he swatted it away. A moment later the fly reappeared, and once again the guy swatted it away. Then, for a third time, the fly buzzed around the guy's backside. Then came the product shot and the tag line: "Hakle. For the Ultimate Cleanliness."

Hakle is a brand of toilet paper.

I am pleased to announce that the joke was so graphic and revolting that the commercial did not win a gold Lion at Cannes. It won a silver Lion.

The jury liked the spot because it was direct and to the point. Yes, it was. So is a knee to the groin. Directness, in and of itself, is no justification for antisocial behavior.

Once again, however, what makes the purveyors of such grossouts so contemptible is not merely their immaturity but their deep cynicism. Because what they know—what they learned at the feet of the master—is that, in the narrowest sense, shockvertising works. It works (a) by provoking widespread outrage, inevitably reported in the press, creating a level of buzz typically outstripping by orders of magnitude the reach of the actual media buy, which buzz (b) bemuses the relatively small target audience. Offend the many, in other words, to impress the few.

There was a time when such a trade-off would have been deemed not merely a bad bargain but anathema to the advertising industry, which for the first century or so of its history believed its first job was to alienate *nobody*. Advertisers often went to extreme lengths dulling and denaturing their own messages, for fear of offending anybody, anywhere. Those weren't necessarily the good old days, but the pendulum hasn't merely swung; it has yanked the advertising world off its axis. The current calculus is the Calvin Klein approach, which has been very bad for advertising, very bad for the culture, and very, very good for Calvin Klein.

When Brooke Shields posed, pantiless, on her back, cooing "Nothing comes between me and my Calvins," people were shocked to hear such sexually suggestive wordplay from the lips of a fifteen-year-old. Then they bought Calvin Klein jeans. When fashion photographer Bruce Weber shot four naked fashion models of various sexes entwined like a can of night crawlers for Obsession fragrance, people were shocked. Then they bought Obsession. When in 1991 Klein took out a 116-page *Vanity Fair* "outsert" filled with Weber's provocative images, including a masturbatory shower scene with the dripping male model and a strategically placed jacket sleeve of, shall we say, stone-washed denim, people were shocked. Then they bought denim. When Klein showed a sixty-square-foot underwear crotch with its contents in water-soaked relief over Times Square, people were shocked. Then they bought Calvin Klein underwear.

Klein, for all practical purposes, invented shockvertising. But he is not an advertiser. He is an arsonist. He lobs Molotov cocktails into the firetrap of the media culture, and moments later the ladder trucks and pumpers of journalism come racing to the scene. This brings the neighbors out to their front porches in their nightclothes to see what all the commotion is about. They stand there appalled, but also somehow titillated, by the conflagration. And while they're out there, gawking, Klein strolls by and sells them millions of dollars worth of CK-branded crap.

His success at this cynical game may be the most poisonous influence on modern advertising. But then, in 1996, in yet one more effort to raise eyebrows and hackles and yet another bonanza of free publicity, he trespassed beyond gratuitousness, beyond titillation, beyond vulgarity to the very core of our moral sensibilities. Calvin Klein, Inc. and in-house agency CRK produced one of the most pro-foundly disturbing campaigns in TV history, a campaign with the look, texture, and nauseating salaciousness of child pornography. And, at long last, Klein paid, withdrawing the ads amid declarations of shock, shock that "some people are taking away a different perception of the ads" from what CK purportedly intended. But, of course—like the ads themselves—such limp apologia were not to be believed.

"You have a lovely body," an unseen middle-aged interviewer was heard saying from the back of a makeshift rumpus room set. The background was cheap Weldwood paneling, the only prop a stepladder on a soiled carpet. The subject was a long-haired teenage boy in a pair of black CK jeans and a black vest but no shirt.

"Mmm-hmm," the boy agreed.

"Do you like your body?" the older man asked.

"Yeah, I like it."

"Mm-hmm. Would you like to see something improved on it?"

"No, I like . . . I like it the way it is."

"[Chuckling] You do?"

"I don't need . . . you know, I don't need all that."

"You don't need to improve it, huh?"

"Uh-uh."

"Well," the interviewer said, leeringly, "those jeans look *real* good on you."

The low production values and audition format apparently mimic the scenario of chickenhawk porn in which children, being interviewed by the unseen "director," are coaxed to disrobe . . . and whatever else. This campaign stops short of nudity and sex acts, but—with boy and girl models alike—it hews to the kiddie porn formula.

"Are you strong?" the older man asked a young James Dean clone in another spot.

"I like to think so."

"Do you think you could rip that shirt off of you? " (And the kid did.)

"That's a nice body. Do you work out?"

"Mmm-hmm."

"[Chuckling] Yeah, I can tell."

In yet another spot, the same narrator tried to get a young girl named Karen to dance. She refused. But a young boy, looking all of fourteen, was happy to "mosh" for the grown-up. It was all just too perverse. The likes of Rev. Donald Wildmon, the sanctimonious, self-appointed arbiter of American moral values, jumped all over Klein and MTV for airing this garbage, but one scarcely needed to be a zealot or a prig to find them irredeemably repugnant. It is one thing to toy with the nation's libido, as Calvin Klein has been doing for two decades. And it is bad enough to glorify and fan the flames of adolescent sexuality. But to portray children as sex toys parading before adults is the line that cannot be crossed.

BOB'S MAILBAG

Sadly (and if you ask me, bizarrely), as I've traveled around the world the last ten years spreading the gospel of common courtesy, the reception to my anger on this subject has been mixed. Occasionally I'm given spontaneous ovations, in recognition of my inspiring moral courage and overall winning personality. Many times, however, I've been challenged, or dismissed with a smug shrug, by the fraternity of all-in-blacks. We've got to break through the clutter, they say. Don't force your conservative standards on me, they say. We're not going to bow to political correctness, they say. Our audience loves this stuff, they say. Our awareness is way up, they say. Have you watched *programming* lately? they say. Lighten up, they say.

Grow up, I say. Wake up, I say. Shut up, I say.

I say it and say it again, to an audience increasingly deaf to reason. Let me just give you an example of the mentality we are up against. What follows is from a letter to *Ad Age* from a reader reacting to a 1994 column much in the vein of this chapter. It managed to encapsulate, in a single stroke, all of the arrogance, illogic, thoughtlessness, and malignant stupidity that is metastasizing through the industry worldwide. I'll leave off the person's name and agency; they've got enough problems. But listen to what this creative director had to say. It explains everything:

> Bob Garfield's commentary on bad ad manners deserves only one headline, three words, with an explanation [sic] point!
>
> Lighten Up Bob!
>
> When I turn on my TV at night to see O.J. updates, crime bill rhetoric, baseball strikes, forced insurance mandates and all the other bad news that network TV has to offer, I find it refreshing to finally see commercials hocking a loogie at morally asinine people like you. My hat's off to Nintendo, Nike, Roy Rogers and especially their agencies for having the guts and great marketing sense to reflect their target market's true attitude and give people like you the finger. If you don't like what's on broadcast TV, get cable and watch the Discovery Channel, Nickelodeon, or that moral majority station with Jerry or just don't watch.

Maybe you could read to your kids or, better yet, buy them
a Nintendo unit, a pair of Nike's and dinner at Roy's.

Welcome to advertising for the nineties Bob, where
everything's fair game. If you don't like it get out.

M.
Creative director

In the face of such gargantuan idiocy, it's almost hard to know
where to begin. But let's start here: "Lighten up." Lighten up? Oh, I
see, the problem is *mine*. I'm just too intolerably blue-nosed. I'm too
sober and serious and spoiling for a fight to just kind of chill and
appreciate the fun of giant-Johnson jokes on prime-time TV. Well,
I'm sorry, *that's* asinine. The issue has nothing to do with me at all.
(In fact, in addition to being omniscient and charming, I personally
can be highly comical. You should see my impressions of Nancy Sina-
tra and Konrad Adenauer. VERY humorous.) No, the issue has to do
solely with those victimized by the excesses of those too callous or
stupid to recognize their own juvenile misfeasance. The "lighten up"
response reminds me of the odious line offered a few years back by
the insufferable basketball coach/fulminating maniac Bobby Knight
about rape: "If rape is inevitable, relax and enjoy it." Ha-ha.

If something is wrong, it's wrong. Laughing along, like children
watching a bully at work on the playground, is just being a cowardly
accessory to the crime.

Furthermore, how conservative I happen to be is utterly beside
the point. The embarrassing fact is I myself can appreciate a penis-
size joke, for example, properly told, in an appropriate setting. I also
managed to suppress my gag reflex enough to see the grim humor in
the PlayStation spot. And, to my taste, the Britches of Georgetown
commercial—the one with the funeral and the casket—is brilliant

and hilarious. That, however, has no bearing on how somebody might feel who had just buried a loved one and turned on the TV only to see a realistic funeral scene devolve into an eternal-death gag.

And there are fifty thousand funerals a week in this country.

That's not an irrelevant statistic. On issues of taste, numbers count, because in what increasingly has become a culture of victimization, almost anything you put on TV has someone or another shouting "How dare they!" In 1988, Roy Rogers Restaurants did a wonderfully nostalgic and very funny look at the frumpy cafeteria ladies of our school days past—only to generate outrage from actual cafeteria workers who felt maligned by the portrayals. The proper corporate response should have been "It's a warm, loving send-up. Deal with it." But Roy Rogers, owned by Marriott Corp., operator of dining services in public schools, cravenly caved and pulled the ad.

Likewise, a 1993 Pepsi commercial depicting a mythical cable TV show on artichoke cooking got an angry response from, yes, the artichoke lobby. And an innocuous PaineWebber spot, which implied the superiority of European piano teachers, was pulled in response to protests from American piano teachers. So, obviously, creatives cannot and should not be daunted by the certain knowledge that whatever they do will offend *someone*. But neither should they use that knowledge to rationalize ideas apt to offend, or anger, or hurt many someones. That's why "Our audience loves this stuff" is also a flimsy excuse. Lots of people love heroin and sadomasochistic porn; shall it be distributed in junior high schools?

Sometimes in advertising it is justified to offend the few to impress the many. It is never justified to offend the many to impress the few.

Yet heaven help anyone who takes legitimate offense, because then come the accusations against the offended party—not just of prudishness, but also of PC. And it's not hard to see why, because virulent inconsideration is not the only negative force at work in the society. There's also the rise of the Thought Police.

The last thirty years have seen the United States surrendering to a culture of the aggrieved wherein an infinite number of put-upon constituencies—from substance abusers to carpal tunnel syndrome sufferers to insulted cafeteria workers—demand financial or judicial or linguistic reparations for some perceived slight to their dignity, the upshot being the ludicrous spectacle of speech codes and multicultural Balkanism. Political correctness is unfortunate in its own right, and I could go on and on. But a secondary tragedy—the collateral damage of political correctness—is the backlash of intolerance for anybody legitimately offended by a genuine affront. To take issue with offensive, rude, inconsiderate behavior nowadays is to be reflexively denounced as just another whining apostle of PC (or, by the whining apostles of PC, as a reactionary, expression-stifling fellow traveler of Jerry Falwell). But once again, the right to be treated courteously has nothing to do with political correctness. What this has to do with is the Golden Rule, which, in addition to being what your mother taught you, is nothing less than the central civilizing principle of mankind. Yet it's a principle so basic, so obvious as to be typically dismissed as puerile. Silly. Outdated. Kids' stuff.

It is not puerile. The Golden Rule is not kids' stuff. It is the fundamental counterbalance to the wanton indulgence of personal impulse and thus the foundation of every nontyranny that has ever prospered in the history of the world.

Is it perhaps time for a reminder that maybe, just maybe, "Do unto others . . . " is worthy of advertising, too?

Of course it is, but the boors are still scoffing, now trotting out their "brand awareness" numbers as evidence of their vision. Which, of course, is a canard. Profitability Hell is populated with the high-profile damned: No Excuses jeans, Benetton, Reebok Pump,

Pets.com, Outpost.com, You-freakin'-name-it.com. Awareness is nothing—at least, nothing of which I'm aware. Charles Manson has fabulous brand awareness. So does anthrax. But nobody's lining up to buy.

FROM THOSE WONDERFUL FOLKS WHO GAVE YOU TOILET CAM

The imperative for self-control is so clear and unassailable it defies rational argument. Yet in the last few years an argument has emerged that imagines itself to be rational, that at first blush may seem compelling, but that in the end collapses as well—namely, that the ends justify the means. Some subjects are of such dire import to the social fabric, proponents maintain, that they may employ any means necessary to shine the bright light of awareness on the issue.

That, of course, is the silly and transparent pretext behind the Benetton campaign. AIDS is such a scourge that Benetton not can but *must* show a corpse, surrounded by grieving relatives, moments after death. The tragedy of the boat people was so grotesque it was Benetton's *duty* to reprint the news photo of refugees clinging to a ship's cargo net like flies to flypaper. The Balkan wars were so murderous it was a *public service* to photograph the bloody uniform of a dead Croatian soldier.

Yeah, it's a fortunate thing the Italian sportswear chain got those pictures out, because otherwise the AIDS pandemic would never have made news. Yeah, lucky us to have been greeted with the shocking antiwar image of the bloody uniform in *Paris Match*. What a stinging rebuke to the pro-war lobby.

It's like, oh, be quiet. Yet many people have been taken in by this campaign, mistaking its belaboring of the painfully obvious for selfless social consciousness. It has been nothing of the kind. Quite the opposite, actually. First of all, the expression of banal ideas—however shockingly presented—can have no effect on the social fabric. It's not as though Benetton, through its courage, has put AIDS or racism or genocide on the world agenda. All Benetton has done through these stunts is win attention for itself on the coattails of searing human tragedy, exploiting and trivializing genuine horrors for the sake of selling overpriced mix-and-match separates to shallow fools. Such behavior is not merely selfish; it is obscene.

In Benetton's case the ends don't justify the means in the first instance because the ends were merely to make Benetton look bold and fearless and cutting edge. But using horrifying images to arouse the apathetic masses is wrong not only in *faux* public-service advertising; it's wrong in genuine public-service advertising as well.

Consider, for example, a 1996 spot from Saatchi & Saatchi, London, for that city's Borough of Islington. The action opened with a man walking cheerfully out of his flat with his morning newspaper. Thereupon, without self-consciousness, he squatted over the sidewalk, tensed his facial muscles (among others) and began to grunt. Yes, as a neighbor lady observed in disgust, and children on the street giggled to witness, he moved his bowels on the street. After finishing his chore he matter-of-factly exchanged a greeting with a passing neighbor, who—unaware of what had just been extruded in front of him—stepped into the fresh deposit, slipping backwards out of the frame.

The payoff: two London-style municipal signs. "You wouldn't," one sign read, and the other: "Don't let your dog." The idea was to jolt careless pet owners into the reality of their fecal irresponsibility—and no doubt this scenario more than did the trick.

There is, however, more to advertising than communication. More than effectiveness. More than memorability. There should have been consideration for viewers who weren't offenders—i.e., the vast majority—and who may have felt as victimized by the repulsive ad as by the doggy land mines themselves. Another Cannes Lion, of course.

No doubt the agency, Jung v. Matt, Hamburg, felt equally right-eous with its year-2000 public-service announcement conceived to discourage cocaine use. It showed an obese, sweating drug mule arriving at an international airport, heading right for the bathroom, and securing a stall. There, thanks to the miracle of Toilet Cam, the viewer got to watch from a distance of six inches as the drug runner evacuated, discharging a condom filled with white powder in a sea of feces. I have nothing to add to the description, nor do I believe it requires further comment, except to say that I wish M., the creative director, could see it on TV every day for the rest of his sad little life.

If perhaps you think this is simply a question of scale—that doggie-doo on the sidewalk and even illegal drug use simply don't rise to the level so distressing to viewers, but that surely a sufficiently horrendous social ill might justify extreme attention-getting meas-ures—I leave you with one more. It was from 2001, a series of PSAs from the United Way of Philadelphia, focusing on the unspeakable cruelty of child abuse.

One spot used grain, docu-style footage to film, from a distance, the window of a city row home. The audio track was the contents of a 911 tape—a real 911 tape—in which a little kid is screaming for help. The father is beating the mother and coming after the child. The reality is not merely chilling; it is unbearable.

Is the cause important? Of course it is. Child-welfare and spousal-abuse agencies deserve to be funded. And those agencies are perfectly within their rights to bring the tragic problem to the atten-tion of an indifferent, or at least otherwise occupied, public. But that does not give them—or anybody—the right to assault viewers with horror. This advertiser, too, feels so righteous: "Do you see what you are turning a deaf ear to?" But, here's the thing. I, as a private indi-vidual, have a right to be distracted. I have a right to be underin-formed. I have a right to bury my head in the sand. I even have a right to shrug and say "Not my problem." My level of social con-sciousness is my business and mine alone. The United Way of Philadelphia itself has every right to try to raise consciousness for its issue. But how dare they barge into my home to torture me, without permission, with more reality than I can bear? How *dare* they? Such advertising exploits not only my emotions but also the victims' pain. It is not charity. It is a cruelty unto itself.

Getting back to the letter, the one with all the "explanation" points. Look, it's also not surprising that frustrated "creative" minds, forced week in and week out to do insipid work for fearful, conser-vative clients, would take vicarious pleasure in seeing their lucky col-leagues expand the frontiers of advertising image making. What's shocking is the letter writer's utter blindness to the notion of com-mon consideration. Isn't it obvious that advertisers have not only a responsibility to mind the sensibilities of readers and viewers but a *special* duty to do so?

Difficult as this may be for many all-in-blacks to get through their thick skulls, once again, advertising is not content. It is not a movie. It is not journalism. It is not programming. It is not editorial matter. It is not a plain-speaking book that announces from the beginning that it will slap you upside the head until it gets your atten-tion. The person encountering an ad has not made one single deci-sion voting for it, in the way, for instance, a reader of daily news columns has voted for the news, come what may, or the viewer of HBO has voted for verisimilitude, come what may, or the listener of the "Howard Stern Show" has voted for outrageousness, come what may, or you have voted for blunt opinions about the ad industry, come what may. That's why it's irrelevant that the "Big Buford" gag is tame next to what comes on every day on the news or on "South Park." The point is, parents can make sure their kids don't watch "South Park." So imagine their reaction when, despite their best efforts to keep a smut-free environment for their children, a hamburger commercial comes on in the middle of say, NFL football, to make that decision for them.

Advertising is unsolicited and uninvited and therefore has particular responsibility for decorum. I mean, what is so complicated about that? What is complicated or ambiguous or debatable about the proposition that it is rude, selfish, boorish, obnoxious, sometimes cruel, and always fundamentally mean to barge into people's homes with material bound to upset them? We've established that you wouldn't invite yourself into strangers' homes to Osterize human tissue. If someone suggested that, as a prank, you call the nice old grandma down the street—or her seven-year-old granddaughter—and talk raunchily about male genitalia, you wouldn't do it. If your neighbor were in mourning for his wife, killed in an automobile accident, you wouldn't knock on his door and tell morbid car-wreck jokes. You wouldn't assemble an auditorium full of teenagers and tell them to dis their parents because life is meaningless anyway. You wouldn't hire models to dress up as a priest and a nun, barge into a Catholic mass, go to the pulpit, and start making out. You wouldn't go to a support group for the families of schizophrenics and act out the bizarre symptoms of psychotic distress. You wouldn't do any of those things, because it would be wrong. It would be upsetting, offensive, traumatic, horrifying to too many people. So why are so many insufferable smart-asses in the industry too arrogant or too stupid to refrain from doing it on TV?

That's meant, of course, to be a rhetorical question, although M., creative director, proposes an answer: if I don't like it, "Don't watch." Ah. As I said, that letter explains everything. Don't watch? Don't watch *what*? If advertising were programming, a viewer could make decisions about what to watch. But—I'll say this one last time—advertising isn't, so a viewer can't, so what's left to watch, if you choose not to be assaulted by advertising, is nothing.

Which destroys the whole medium, you imbecile.

CHAPTER 7

ARE YOU DOOMED? TAKE THIS SIMPLE QUIZ!

There's this Yugoslavian movie. It's called *Underground*, by Emir Kusturica, and it is a classic of Eastern European cinema. The film begins in Belgrade during World War II. The city is being bombed in advance of the German occupation. A group of smugglers takes refuge in a huge cellar to wait out the siege. There, over an extended period, they develop an increasingly sophisticated subterranean society. Meanwhile, only one of them ever goes up to the surface to scope out the situation, returning periodically to inform his comrades about the bleak circumstances above. Between what food and raw materials their intrepid spy manages to supply them and what they have fashioned in the cellar, they survive for thirty years.

They are extremely resourceful, extremely ingenious, and immensely proud of their achievement.

Only one problem: the Germans were routed by the Allies in 1944. The undergroundlings' sleazy friend has misled them the whole time. While he double-dealt himself into riches and power above ground, they have languished in their hole, oblivious. They imagined one kind of world above them and finally surfaced to discover quite another. Chaos ensued.

OK, now. Hold that thought.

Before resuming the history of Balkan cinema, let's just take a brief moment to recall some television commercials. The first crossed my desk in 1986. It came with a press release boasting about an enormous production budget employed in service of what it termed a communications "breakthrough." The secret of this particular breakthrough was the science of semiotics—i.e., conveying meaning via powerful symbols imbued with significance far beyond their literal interpretation. It's the sort of thing that Jean Baudrillard and Noam Chomsky write about. Umberto Eco. Dudes like that, dudes who have no direct responsibility for market share.

"Whoa," I said to myself as I eagerly tore the videocassette out of its jacket. "This is gonna suck."

Yes, I jumped to conclusions, but not out of arrogance or ill temper. This was experience speaking. Most of the worst ads I have ever seen were FedExed to me by their creators, completely unsolicited, accompanied by breathless press releases about such-and-such a "breakthrough." So, yes, I girded myself for a debacle, but of course I was prepared to be pleasantly surprised. The spot was titled "Evolution." It opened with a shot of caveman, a bearded Neanderthal with a funky loincloth and all kinds of back hair, running along a glacial canyon. Running, running, running. The viewer knew not why, but this refugee of prehistory was running his furry loins off. Somehow he found himself atop a cliff, but, as he sprinted forward, there facing him was a gaping crevasse, too wide to leap.

Watching all of this, a viewer had to think, Ah, so that's how the Missing Link went missing. But, no, this fellow jumped anyway—a long soaring leap. And while he was in the air, in extreme close-up and superslow motion, naturally he turned into an astronaut.

In a spacesuit, space walking. With a smile. And a salute.

If you're expecting that there was accompanying copy to connect the narrative dots, you are forgetting that this was a semiotic breakthrough. The people who spent a quarter million 1986 dollars to create this breakthrough were conveying meaning via powerful symbols imbued with significance far beyond their literal interpretation. All that this ad supplied to finish its sell was a logo and voice-over tag line:

"Perpetual. Where your bank is going to be."

Yep, it was a bank commercial—a local bank commercial, no less. Strangely, however—though the ad clearly conveyed meaning via powerful symbols imbued with significance far beyond their literal meaning—it did not win a basketful of awards trophies and adoration for all involved. What it won was widespread disbelief and ridicule. Still, as perhaps the press-release writer imagined, a great deal did in fact occur as a direct and indirect result of this world-class example of pretentious, silly creative self-indulgence.

The agency, Athey Martin Webb, Richmond, Virginia, lost the account.

The agency went out of business.

The bank failed.

"Perpetual" nothing. The tag line should have been "Transitory. What your bank is going to be."

Hence:

Reality Check No. 1: Do you really think consumers are sitting there waiting for a Breakthrough?

They aren't. Do not be so blindly determined to "think outside the box" that you are constructing your own coffins.

Yet it happens all the time, because, I have long suspected, of a fundamental misunderstanding by advertising people about what they do for a living. Here's another commercial, from 1988: Picture five weary schlubs trudging to an open elevator car, their heads bowed, their shoulders stooped, at day's end not only exhausted but defeated. The background music: the dismal minor chords, way down-tempo of "The Volga Boatman."

Then imagine the elevator doors closing to reveal, of course . . . a giant Campbell's Soup label. Yep, and now picture the doors reopening to a new musical background: the upbeat "Mmm-mmm good" theme. And what has happened to the five weary riders? They seem to have disappeared, until the camera pans down to reveal . . . babies! The bone-tired adults have turned into babies. Smiling, cooing babies. Then the voice-over: "At the end of a long day, a hot bowl of Campbell's Soup can make you feel . . . like new again."

René Magritte, eat your heart out. Enigma meets condensed-soup marketing. "We wanted to make it very simple but at the same time evoke a warm sense of nostalgia through the use of symbolism," a Backer Spielvogel Bates, New York, executive explained in a press release. "The five adults, for example, aren't five people but rather the entire world. The actual eating of the soup is conveyed through the closing of the elevator doors."

Ah, yes. Of course it is. And the beige tones of the elevator's interior panels symbolize either death, castration, or "We hope you like sodium." I'm not sure which. Any way you shake it, this guy has read wayyyyyy too much Nathaniel Hawthorne.

All right, maybe that was a low blow, because the agency's idea of using nonverbal imagery to flesh out the regenerative powers of hot soup wasn't, in and of itself, a terrible idea. The charge of the Light Brigade, that was a terrible idea. The Watergate break-in was a terrible idea. Noxzema for Dishes was a terrible idea. The Campbell's spot was a satisfactory idea, executed terribly—like the Iran hostage rescue mission and the O.J. prosecution.

Still, there must be a better way to symbolize soup's warm vitality than an elevator full of babies—an image that suggests not regeneration so much as . . . I don't know . . . Campbell's Baby Soup? It was ambitious; I'll give them that. And it was extremely, extremely arty. In fact it was exactly the kind of artiness, as we recall from Chapter 2, that makes people hate art. But it was also completely unnecessary, because—and I'm sorry to deliver such terrible news—advertising isn't art.

Reality Check No. 2: Do you think that because you're called a "writer" or an "art director," you're an artist?

If you do, you are sadly and dangerously mistaken. Advertising uses artistic tools, and it needs to use them well, but fundamentally it isn't art at all. It is commerce. It is there for one reason only: to sell stuff to folks.

Hard to say which foray into artful symbolism was more mind-boggling in its semipsychotic semiotics, but at least in Perpetual's defense, it's not all that hard to see how a bank can find itself reaching for something different. Before agency creative departments ever go to work fashioning campaigns, they usually do some sort of attitudinal research, and they always—without exception—find the same thing: people don't like banks. They find them impersonal, bureaucratic, greedy, uncaring, and clueless on the most basic techniques of customer service. The result is that about 90 percent of bank advertising from about 1960 reiterated the list of grievances and claimed, one way or another, "We're different."

Of course, until the late eighties, when many branches started keeping normal hours—versus those ridiculous close-at-3:00 banker's hours—and bank-by-phone became simple, and various other innovations took root, it was all a big lie. Nobody's bank was different, and the consumer resentment grew and grew. Of course, what bank-by-phone did for consumer trust was not quite enough to compensate for the savings-and-loan crisis, a $150 billion fiasco brought on by the largest financial fraud in the history of commerce. (See Chapter 8, "Hold the Sleaze, Please.") And just about the time the government wrote the last check to undo the damage, Congress changed the law about interstate banking. Soon the smoldering ruins of Perpetual were acquired by Crestar, which was subsequently acquired by SunTrust, which—at this writing—was facing a takeover by Wachovia. Elsewhere, American Bank of Pennsylvania became Meridian, which was acquired by CoreStates, which was acquired by First Union. And so on. Suddenly banks were no longer perceived as uncaring and impersonal. They were obscenely voracious, uncaring, and impersonal. Cultivating a nice, personal customer relationship with Citibank was like cultivating a nice, personal relationship with the Pentagon.

In such an environment, talking about lobby hours in your ads cannot be expected to break through the wall of consumer uncertainty and suspicion.

This brings us to another example, a campaign for that very voracious financial leviathan, First Union. Understanding that the clichés of the genre had long since lost relevance to the customers, the client decided to establish an entirely different idiom for the category. Thus, in 1998, amid much fanfare, did the merger-created colossus unveil two extraordinarily gothic commercials. Contrived by Publicis & Hal Riney in San Francisco and produced by Industrial Light & Magic—George Lucas's digital-effects house—the ads marshaled all manner of computer whizbangery to create a setting, and a mood, that seemed lifted directly from Tim Burton's *Batman*. The introductory spot began with a voice-over belonging to the mellifluous Hal Riney himself.

"This is a world only a few know well, a world of risk and uncertainty, where the roads can take you to success or prosperity—or sometimes, to no place at all. This is the financial world."

This wasn't the typical Riney soft-shoe of the sort that had graced commercials for everyone from Ronald Reagan to Subway sandwich shops. And no wonder. The accompanying imagery was straight from hell. Onscreen: a hard, dark, deeply disturbing vision of the financial landscape, a dusky city illuminated like a carnival midway by garish neon and a population of grotesques. Fire-breathers. Fortune-tellers. Painted-faced freaks. Anxious customers grasping but never reaching. When one of them fell to the ground, his face shattered into shards.

"For decades," Riney continued, "banks and investment firms of mountainous size have ruled the land. Yet high above the horizon, another mountain has risen—a mountain called First Union, with sixteen million customers, the nation's eighth-largest brokerage and sixth-largest bank."

Here, like an instantaneous geological outcropping, erupted a towering glass First Union edifice, leaving all the city in its imposing shadow.

"For a new perspective of the financial world, come to a mountain called First Union. Or, if you prefer, the mountain will come to you."

No, no. Please. Not necessary. FOR GOD'S SAKE, STAY RIGHT WHERE YOU ARE!

A surreal oppressive landscape in the shadow of a looming corporate monolith . . . hmmm . . . isn't that more or less everything the public fears and loathes in financial institutions? As I was saying, for years banks have been telling us they're the good friends and neighbors next door, which, of course, is nonsense. But so is positioning yourself as the Prince of Financial Darkness. First Union's bizarre, unearthly TV debut verged on the suicidal.

Granted, the advertiser had its eye on big trust-department clients and investment-bank deals, versus retail banking. And the

First Union "mountain" somewhat recalled Prudential's famed Rock of Gibraltar. But the Rock is synonymous with stability and permanence—not arrogance, distance, cold indifference, or excessive accumulation of wealth, influence, and power. In service of its stated goal to quickly become a household name, First Union paid in excess of $1 million per spot—before a penny was even spent on media—to conjure every negative emotion imaginable.

Please note: Satan is a household name. It's just that nobody wants to do business with him.

Sure enough, the results were remarkable. When the campaign broke, First Union shares sold for $70. When the client finally killed the ads, shares sold for $30. If you're scoring at home, and multiplying by the number of common shares then outstanding, that means this campaign cost the client $36 billion. I will wager my Richie Ashburn autographed baseball, however, that it is still on the creative director's résumé reel.

Reality Check No. 3: Are you so lost in the funhouse of the production process, too pumped full of creative adrenaline, to see how your elaborate dream might materialize as the viewers'—and the client's—worst nightmare?

Nobody in the eventual audience will care about how complicated and exciting the project was.

Just as we said in the introduction: myopia by immersion. We look, but we do not see. Consider a 2000 campaign from DDB, Chicago, for JCPenney. To promote the campaign in the media, Penney's sent out black T-shirts, manufactured in scenic El Salvador, with its new tag line, "it'sallinside," printed on the front and the chain's logo on the back. Yeah, nice start. As if anyone would be seen in public in such a thing. As if Penney's logo, by sheer corporate will, was somehow going to be transformed from the very definition of déclassé to a badge of cool. While the Gap may have enough cachet to persuade its customers to be walking billboards, JCPenney never will. May we repeat that? N-e-v-e-r w-i-l-l. Among the chains with a stronger claim to fashionability are Arthur Treacher's Fish 'n' Chips, Mail Boxes Etc., and Muffler King. Yet the spots, in dead earnest, went on to portray what Penney's called a new concept of women's wear.

"The days when fashion can dictate what women wear," the company asserted in its press materials, "are over." Mmm-hmm. Sure they were. Compared to that, Neville Chamberlain's "Peace in our time" was a prophecy of doom, because wishful thinking does not a marketing plan make. But, I'll give them this: if that postfashion era materializes, JCPenney is extremely well positioned.

Another sterling example, from the same agency in the same year, was for McDonald's. In many ways the new work was a successor to "You deserve a break today" and other classic DDB-McDonald's collaborations of the past. It was cheerful, upbeat, and filled with the heartwarming slice-of-life stuff we've grown so accustomed to. Most important, the theme, "We love to see you smile!" was a worthy reflection of the brand's legacy and a true synthesis of its four core principles: service, cleanliness, friendliness, and value. Furthermore, the tag line was technically true; McDonald's does love to see us smile. It's the ultimate validation of founder Ray Kroc's philosophy.

The problem was, it was a pipe dream. Today's McDonald's experience is nothing even minimally reflective of Kroc's core values. By 2000, service, cleanliness, and friendliness had utterly deteriorated. The company made a lot of noise about increased training of its six hundred thousand employees, but as the spot aired it was far away from instilling service values among its crews. The full-employment economy of that time only made matters worse, providing as a hiring base those who hitherto had ranged from marginal to hard-core unemployable.

That, of course, was a force beyond the chain's control. But it was also a situation the company has greatly exacerbated by not policing—or even cutting loose—franchisees who failed to enforce standards. In any event, whatever or whoever may have been to blame for the notorious McDonald's Unhappy Meal, the campaign made a great mistake, because to anyone who has ever had a Big Mac flung at them by a sullen counter clerk—i.e., everyone—it rang so preposterously false.

The commercials were sweet (and so was the wonderful, grin-enhanced Golden Arches logo), but the promise was simply laughable. If you advertise smiles and don't deliver smiles, what you will get first is frowns. Then you'll get abandoned for Wendy's.

How many advertisers learned that lesson the hard way? From Chevrolet to K Mart to Holiday Inn to United to "This is not your father's Oldsmobile," we've seen the folly of premature self-congratulation. The unfortunate truth was, when the campaign aired, the chain had long since stopped being your father's McDonald's. With its daunting training challenge, the stagnancy of same-store growth, and the unfavorable valuation of the euro (which at that moment was decimating its European profits), the company had enough problems. The last thing it needed was McBacklash.

So, I guess they were a little mad at me when I offered them a little jingle to go along with the campaign:

> *Forget the smile. Forget the laughs.*
> *We ring you up with pictographs.*
> *The floor is filthy. The toilet's worse.*
> *We're the rudest in the universe.*

You want happy? Just kiss our butts.
We take your cash but hate your guts.
The closest thing to "Thanks!" you'll get
Is an outstretched hand and a Beanie pet.

Chorus: Smile! We're in denial. We think saying it must
  make it true.
What we love to see is same-store sales, so we're lying to
  ourselves and you!

Yeah, they got mad at me, and took my criticism quite personally, but soon enough the slogan was contracted merely to "Smile."

Reality Check No. 4: Do you really believe that wishing makes it so?

If your advertising premise makes the audience snort with derision at your ridiculously idealized vision of the brand, you will do
more harm than good.

Remember how, way back in the Introduction, I bragged how
I'm never wrong? Then I qualified it by saying that one time out of
a hundred even I—the anointed one—can screw up. Well, here's a
doozy. In 1997, in advance of the International Advertising Film Festival, I wrote about the best commercial in the world that year. It
was from Delvico Bates, Barcelona, for Esencial hand cream, and
it just blew me away. The action opened with a pretty young woman
riding her bicycle on a country lane, a pastoral tableau marred only
by the persistent squeak of the bike's unlubricated chain. Irritated
by the noise, the woman dismounted, reached into her bag, and produced a jar of Esencial. Then she opened the jar, took a wad of
cream, and rubbed it onto the chain. Then she rode away. Squeak
squeak squeak.

The noise didn't disappear. Why? Because, as the voice-over explained, "Esencial moisturizes, but it has no grease."

What a pure advertising idea: a problem/resolution spot where the brand pointedly cannot solve the problem! It was, in other words, a vivid demonstration of brand nonattributes. Inspired. Cunning. Brilliant.

Right? No, wrong. Wildly, embarrassingly wrong, because Esencial hand cream did not exist. It was a *trucho*, a ghost, a fake commercial, entered to fetch a gold Lion—which, with the help of my crusade on its behalf, it unfortunately did. Shame on them. Shame on Cannes. Shame on me.

Reality Check No. 5: Are you believing your fictions?

A "ghost" ad is not an ad. There is no "director's cut." There is no gem the client didn't approve. There is no :60 if the media buy pays for only :30s. They do not exist. The only advertising that exists is that which the consumer sees. Period.

Look, mistakes are made. Things happen. Everybody's life and career at some point crashes head-on into the Law of Unintended Consequences. The purpose of our inquiry is simply to figure out why, in advertising, this seems to happen so often. And soon enough I'll take a stab at that, but for now you might take comfort in the fact that it happens to everybody. Everybody. Even me. Even Nike.

This is a company that, in partnership mainly with Wieden & Kennedy, Portland, Oregon, has converted four simple insights into a $100 billion industry. The first, by founder Phil Knight, was that stylish, technologically superior athletic shoes could be sold at high margins with the help of sophisticated, inspiring advertising. The second was Knight's vision of "owning" sport—its power, its emotion, its excitement, its grit, its drama, its glory. Nike, he knew, could make its brand stand for all that sport encompasses. The third was

Wieden's formulation "Just do it," a harsh admonition bordering on the rude that happened to inspire and empower millions of people worldwide to get off the sofa and do what the furry caveman did, minus the supernatural conversion to the space program. And the fourth was the endorsement contract with Michael Jordan.

Some people take advertising advice from God. Others sign Him to a long-term deal.

In sum, Nike did more than any advertiser since Marlboro cigarettes to make its marketing the essence of its product. Advertising didn't simply add value; it represented the majority of the value in any given garment bearing the Nike swoosh.

All of which is to say these aren't bunglers we're speaking of. Yet, during the 2000 Summer Olympics in Sydney, Nike and Wieden contrived to make a witty observation about the benefits of sport and wound up in the center of a scandal.

The spot featured American track-and-field Olympian Suzy Favor Hamilton running in terror from a chainsaw-wielding psychopath. The hulking attacker, looking very much like the horror-movie menace Freddy Krueger, was seen surprising her in her house and chasing her into the woods, with obviously murderous intent. But Hamilton, world-class athlete, easily outran him. The punch line: "Why sport? Because you'll live longer."

Ha. Ha. Ha. The attempt to lampoon the teen-horror genre was so vivid and scary that it was widely derided as a perversity, a sick joke trivializing violence against women. One viewer, quoted in the *New York Times*, called the commercial "truly disgusting and misogynistic." This would have been bad enough if those involved had been so caught up in their own cleverness and sense of black comedy that they simply—as in the First Union debacle—never considered the potential for backlash. Astonishingly, though, in this case an agency spokeswoman said the incensed reaction had been "somewhat expected." And yet they proceeded anyway, placing their client's priceless image at unnecessary risk, and their own reputation as well. That's pretty much the definition of hubris, a quality guaranteed eventually to destroy you. The spot happened to overlap revelations about the Asian sweatshops manufacturing Nike shoes and the company's fortunes plummeted.

Reality Check No. 6: Are you so persuaded of your own infallibility to imagine you are immune to the judgments of the outside world?

Think about the advice they give roofers and iron workers. You've got to feel comfortable up there, or else you'll fall. But you can't feel *too* comfortable, or else you'll forget where you are . . . and fall.

The Nike blunder is an amazing story, and a suitably cautionary tale, but when it comes to raw obliviousness, when it comes to a runway fashion show for the Emperor's New Sneakers, there is nothing—and most likely never will be again—quite like Just for Feet.

This was in 1998. Just for Feet was a fast-growing retailer of athletic shoes eager to establish its brand nationally while simultaneously generating store traffic with a giveaway promotion. What, specifically, the company planned to give away was a new Hummer ground-assault-sized sport utility vehicle. It asked its agency, Saatchi & Saatchi, Rochester, New York, to come up with a commercial that would achieve brand building and promote the promotion at the same time. The result was unforgettable, in approximately the way passing a kidney stone is unforgettable.

The commercial opened on a long-distance runner training, barefoot, over a vast expanse of Kenyan veldt. Next in the picture was a Humvee, or at least a civilian Hummer painted in desert camouflage, with five white occupants dressed for combat, apparently tracking the runner across the plain. Amid much commotion, they succeeded in sighting him, overtaking him, subduing him, and drugging him. Upon eventually awakening, the poor runner found himself shod—against his will and in arrogant defiance of centuries of Kenyan tradition—in Just for Feet sneakers.

The client had some reservations about the commercial at various points in its conception and production, but the agency—in the frozen grip of The Creative Process—assured the clueless suits that this was a humorous way to dramatize the brand's growing reach. How shocked they must have been after the spot finally aired and the firestorm began. The commercial was so violent, so neocolonialist, so fundamentally racist, and—oh, by the way—so bizarrely oblique in its sales pitch that the client had to pull it immediately and apologize that it had ever seen the light of day.

Fortunately for the advertiser, the Humvee spot aired only once. And, really, how many people watch the Super Bowl?

Yes, the Super Bowl. This was Saatchi's idea for breaking through the clutter. I actually saw the ad the Friday before the game and—for only the second time in twenty years—called the agency to see if they really intended to air such a monstrosity. Yeah, they said, "We're very excited about it." They were so very, very excited about it they spent $2 million of the client's money for the slot on the big game, another $900,000 on the production, and $800,000 or so on the Hummer promotion. This spot, they were certain, would leave a lasting impression.

Oh, it left an impression. In the aftermath of the publicity nightmare that ensued, the client eventually became so impressed and so excited that it filed a malpractice lawsuit against the agency: "As a direct consequence of Saatchi's appallingly unacceptable and shockingly unprofessional performance, Just for Feet's favorable reputation has come under attack, its reputation has suffered, and it has been subjected to the entirely unfounded and unintended public perception that it is a racist or racially insensitive company." At this writing, the litigation was still pending. But the lesson is clear:

Reality Check No. 7: When someone raises a red flag, do you think it means "Proceed with caution"?

No, it means "Stop."

Those are seven questions to consider at every stage of producing advertising. But that doesn't mean dog-earing this page and referring to it often. It means building into the creative process mechanisms for checking reality at every stage. As we have long since established, it is so very easy to be so caught up in the process that you utterly lose perspective—kind of like those wretches who get lost in the woods and walk in circles, for want of a compass or a reference point on the horizon—until they finally keel over and die. So, what I'm saying is, don't walk in circles until you keel over and die. Before you venture into the woods, establish a reference point of reality outside of the agency and keep it always in view. One solution: focus groups.

Not because focus groups constitute actual "research." They don't. In fact, because they consist of a statistically meaningless sample and can be manipulated by their leaders or mouthy alpha male participants, focus groups can be *antithetical* to research, leading "researchers" to exactly the wrong conclusion. What focus groups mostly are is a pacifier for suckers who think they are witnessing data in real time. Alas, what they are witnessing is not data at all. It's blather, which is often interesting but which can be generated just as easily, at no cost, at Thanksgiving dinner or the hairdresser.

All that said, though, focus groups can be useful for monitoring campaigns in progress. Why? Because one of the morons whom you have scientifically recruited by molesting them in the mall next to the Orange Julius stand may say something worth listening to. Something like "That's obnoxious." Or "How dare you!" Or "I don't go to the mall to decode a condensed-soup message." Or "A smile at McDonald's? That's a hot one." Or, simply, "I don't get it." That's not data, but it's sure as hell worth investigating. You don't need statistically significant data to stumble on an insight, especially if the insight is: this commercial sucks.

(There was a moment a few years back when I myself, contemplating the inexhaustible supply of business opportunities, even considered leaving journalism and renting myself out to clients as a one-man reality check. Briefly, visions of dollar signs danced in my head. Then I did my own reality check and realized I'd rather pour Liquid-Plumr on my eyeballs.) But it doesn't particularly matter what mechanism an agency and its client employ to prevent such debacles as this chapter so gruesomely describes, only that there is one. Asking the spouse and kids is better than nothing. It's far better than nothing. The only key is that, whichever outside source you consult, you listen. Listen carefully. Don't roll your eyes and dismiss the negative, because if you do, in due course, that's exactly what your target audience will do with you.

By the way, back to Kusturica's cinema masterpiece. When the tiny subterranean society finally emerges at the surface, they stumble on the on-location set of a film of their own story—a film that idealizes them as guerrilla heroes. They mistake the on-camera action for reality and launch into the military action for which they've prepared for decades. In the ensuing helter-skelter, blood is shed, friends turn on one another, and the country is ruined. Their goal had been to alter the course of history, and, in apocalyptic ways they never imagined from the unreality of their bunker, that is precisely what they did.

HOLD THE SLEAZE, PLEASE

Funny thing about Republicans. They're very big on law and order when it involves keeping the teeming hoi polloi under control but philosophically (and very nearly pathologically) against government regulation of business. This often has deleterious consequences, when solid citizens with multiple residences and expensive neckties team with lobbyists and pricey lawyers to lie, cheat, and plunder. Let's flash back to the period between 1982 and 1990, shall we? That's when—and I say this with all respect—scheming, thieving, scum-sucking vermin like Michael Milken and Charles Keating took advantage of dearly bought deregulatory changes in federal law to loot the savings and loan industry and its millions of innocent depositors of $150 billion. It was the largest financial crime in the history of the world.

It was also, as investment frauds tend to be, quite technical and complicated. The methods were so arcane, and the dollar figures so unimaginable, the press was at a loss to cover the story in terms readers could grasp, much less be outraged by. In newspapers around the country, reporters spent years trying to document and explain the scale of the fraud, but their efforts typically were relegated to the business section, the inside pages of the news section, or, if they happened to miraculously land on page one, below the fold, next to the latest unread installment on campaign-finance reform. It wasn't until 1993 that *The Washington Post* ran an S&L-scandal story stripped across the entire top of the front page. It concerned the Resolution Trust Corp., the federal agency chartered to bail out the beleaguered thrifts:

"RTC Pays $35 an Hour for Photocopying Files; Probe Faults Multimillion-Dollar Contract"

The RTC, it turned out, was paying ridiculous sums to photocopy documents, resulting in overcharges to the government and, therefore, to the taxpayer. Predictably, the public was enraged. The radio talk shows were abuzz. An investigation was mounted. And, sure enough, a federal audit was able to document overcharges totaling in excess of $15,000.

$15,000.

One one-hundred-thousandth of the cost of the S&L fiasco.

It's like a $700 military toilet seat buried in a trillion-dollar federal budget. Anger comes easily over scandals we think we understand. History repeated itself in the Enron debacle, when a gang of church-going, Hermès-wearing, charity-endowing crooks cooked the books with a confusing array of offshore partnerships, transforming Enron first from an old-economy pipeline company into a high-flying, modern airship of deregulation, then finally into a financial *Hindenberg*. The $600 million in hidden losses barely pierced the public consciousness. Only when employees lost $50,000-a-year jobs and retirement assets did the scandal break through the headlines for the human catastrophe it was.

And so it is in advertising, where every so often a high-profile misdeed is unearthed. Someone at BBDO has put marbles on the bottom of the soup bowl, to make Campbell's seem denser with vegetable goodness. Someone at the production company has welded reinforcing I-beams beneath the roof of the Volvo to gird it against crushing in the dramatic roof-strength demo. Some smart-aleck political consultant semisubliminally flashes the word *RATS* in an otherwise merely nasty attack ad. Someone—Cybill Shepherd, let's say—is caught endorsing red meat while privately refusing to eat it.

And every time something like this happens, people go "Aha! Just as we always knew! It's a sleazy business, rooted in dishonesty."

Even within the industry, these incidents always trigger an uproar, and with it a spate of nervous hand-wringing about the integrity of advertising. OK. Fine. The industry should certainly concern itself with its integrity, but souped-up soup is hardly the bogeyman. Advertising's real shames aren't isolated cases of behind-the-scenes cheating. The big scandals are, like the savings-and-loan crisis was for years before the public caught on, larger and ongoing.

Chapter 6 documented one such: the alarming trend toward shockvertising. Another is political advertising, which rancid stain on democracy I won't discuss very much here, because it is perpetrated generally not by the ad industry, per se, but by Washington political consultants, who make tobacco lobbyists look, comparatively speaking, like the Dalai Lama. Then there is sexism, which, as we also have seen, bubbles up from time to time and sometimes even erupts volcanically. Those are the high-profile scourges. But there are more, scourges that go on in advertising all the time yet hardly ever seem to register on the government regulators' radar, much less the public's. Let's start with an obvious one: dishonesty.

JOE ISUZU, ROLE MODEL

In a November 2001 tracking poll by the Gallup Organization rating the honesty and ethical behavior of various professions, firefighters (in the immediate aftermath of the World Trade Center attacks) ranked first with 90 percent of respondents judging them high or very high in integrity. Then came nurses, members of the U.S. military, police, druggists, and physicians. Next, at 64 percent, were clergy. Journalists, at 29 percent, were squeezed between bankers and congressmen. Lawyers came in at 18 percent. Insurance salesmen at 13 percent.

Advertising professionals, I am pleased to report, did not come in dead last. Car salesmen came in dead last, with 8 percent. Advertising professionals—at 11 percent—were next to last. Just below insurance agents. That's *below* insurance agents.

Congratulations. In all fairness, neither terrorists nor their evil cousins, podiatrists, were on the list, so the odds were stacked against advertising. But considering that rigged-Volvo incidents don't come around too often, it's worth investigating the reason for such universal suspicion and disrespect.

If you wish to be defensive, of course, you can always turn back to Chapter 5 for the explanation: people are stupid. Clearly, some of the public's distaste for the industry is rooted in a sort of brainless conventional wisdom: you're *supposed* to equate advertising with trickery. Caveat emptor and all that. Even if the respondents don't actually have cause to hold the industry in contempt, they know they're free to say they do. It's like complaining about the TV weatherman. It sounds like an actual opinion, and it will never go challenged. And if it were to be challenged, it takes only one unforecast blizzard—or, say, one Cybill Shepherd dietary revelation—to end the discussion.

That, however, is just part of the explanation. The other part is the industry's long and frequently inglorious history of puffery, deception, and sleazy half-truths, some of which persist even today. There is some good news in that such behavior, while it persists, does not prevail. Because in the modern era the major media are fairly vigilant, and because national advertisers fear getting hauled into federal court by competitors, the days of naked deceit for the vast majority of national-advertising categories are substantially over. What lingers in certain categories, though, is the systematic purveyance of half-truths—the cunning assembly of nominal facts leading the consumer inevitably to a false conclusion. In long-distance telephone service, wireless service, automobile leasing, credit cards, and department-store promotions, consumers have learned the hard way to assume that the great deal trumpeted in the headline is belied by restrictions, exceptions, hidden costs, and financial traps buried in the fine print (or John Moschita–like fast-talking audio disclaimer). Maybe you shrug and say "Oh, well, that's *retail* advertising; it's not the same as branding." Actually, I know for a fact people say that, because a famous advertising guy—Sean "Heartbeat of America" Fitzpatrick, former vice chairman of McCann-Erickson Worldwide— wrote as much in my own publication.

"The public is exposed to a large portion of trash that goes by the name of advertising," now-*Professor* Fitzpatrick wrote in February 2002. "It looks like advertising. It sounds like advertising. . . . You and I know that it is not *our* advertising."

We do, do we? Hey, Sean is a nice guy, and it's heartening to see him want to separate the lofty brand builders from the carpet merchants, but he has left Madison Avenue only to set up shop in Denial World. Take my word for it, consumers see all advertising as advertising because all advertising *is* advertising—which is why every inadequately disclosed $2,900 "cash-on-signing" for a $209-per-month car lease eventually undercuts the credibility of Colgate-Palmolive and Hyatt Hotels and Subway and Ameritrade, too. Sean's modest proposal is to brand brand advertising with a sort of American Association of Advertising Agencies, American Advertising Federation, Association of National Advertisers joint seal of approval.

Oh, *that* would set minds to rest.

I have a better idea. Let the AAAA and the AAF and the ANA demand honesty from everybody.

The advertising industry has reflexively cringed at government regulation by the Federal Trade Commission and the Food and Drug Administration, lobbying instead for the glacial, toothless, and basically irrelevant "self-regulation" of the National Advertising Division of the Council of Better Business Bureaus. The federal government has more or less cooperated, too, since the end of the Jimmy Carter administration, by substantially dismantling its advertising-regulation apparatus and ceding responsibility to the NAD and the courts. This is a bad bargain. Ask Rudy Giuliani, who understood that crime goes down when there are more cops on the beat making life miserable for minor offenders. A few good government crackdowns would sting at first and thereafter have exactly the chilling effect the industry fears, the eventual upshot of which would be an end to chronic, blatant abuses that tar not just the scummy perpetrators but all advertisers, all the time. In other words—via approximately the same mechanism as Rudy's New York Miracle—a huge boon, over time, to the industry's reputation and the credibility of its messages. And bad news for insurance salesmen everywhere.

THERE ARE LIES, DAMNABLE LIES, AND SINUS REMEDIES

Now then, I said I wouldn't dwell on political advertising, and I won't, but let's look there for a moment to see the problem in crystalline purity.

In 1999, late in the campaign for a Virginia legislative seat, the Democratic incumbent, Ken Plum, was leading his Republican challenger, Mike Pocalyko. Plum was leading in spite of his consistent—and consistently unpopular—position against the death penalty. Among bills he voted against were ones mandating death for adults convicted of sexual crimes against children. Plum favored life in prison without parole.

In the last week before the election, Pocalyko decided to call Plum's record on this issue to the attention of the voters in Virginia's thirty-sixth legislative district. He did so with flyers mailed to every voter's home. The headline: "Who Voted to Protect Child Molesters Who Murder Children?"

The message was printed in blood-red ink, complete with little spatter marks around the type, all beneath a giant blood stain, itself containing an image of a little girl being approached by a pervert. "All we wanted to do was get you to open the brochure," the candidate later explained. He lost.

We can certainly agree that such manipulation of information is sick and reprehensible, yet here's the scary part: it was accomplished using nothing but "facts." How? Because there is a difference between fact and truth. In this example the parts may be themselves true, but the whole is a filthy, preposterous, reckless, cynical, shameless, damnable lie. It is also standard operating procedure in political campaigns, run by opportunistic dirty tricksters such as would make Machiavelli blush.

And regular advertising does it, too. Especially food advertising. For instance, a 1997 campaign from Foote, Cone & Belding, New York, for Planter's mixed nuts. The commercial was set on a desert island, where a castaway and his chimpanzee companion are ecstatic over food crates unexpectedly washing ashore.

"Planter's nuts!" the hungry man cries. He quickly pulls out a can of nuts and starts to eat but then has second thoughts: "Actually, Cootchie," he says to the chimp, "perhaps we shouldn't. We have to watch what we eat." But, no, the chimp points out, check out the label.

"All this good stuff, and no cholesterol?!" the castaway exclaims. "Cootchie, to the lounge chairs!" Whereupon, on the beach, they feast on mixed nuts. Meanwhile, superimposed type appears at the bottom of the screen: "A cholesterol-free food. Fourteen grams of fat per serving." (Actually, the label says 16 grams, which means that nuts are 55 percent fat.) Then the voice-over: "Planter's nuts. Fresh roasted taste, no cholesterol. Planter's. Relax. Go nuts."

Sure—why not? What do the marketers at Nabisco care if you clog your arteries?

While no advertiser bears the responsibility for warning consumers away from high-fat products, Planter's has no business portraying snack food as "good stuff." First of all, as to the central proposition, eating cholesterol-laden products, per se, isn't a big issue. Most harmful blood cholesterol—as Nabisco well understands—is produced by the body itself from the saturated fat content of foods. Therefore, to prevent such blatant misdirection, FDA guidelines permit a no-cholesterol claim only if total saturated fat per serving is less than 20 percent of the maximum recommended daily value. Mixed nuts have total fat per serving of 24 percent of the RDV, but on saturated fat they come in at 11 percent—technically qualifying for the no-cholesterol claim.

That's if you buy that one ounce constitutes a realistic "serving." One ounce is a small handful. Two handfuls would go well beyond the 20 percent threshold and take up 48 percent of the daily recommended fat intake. But put that aside for a moment, because dubious serving sizes are hardly the point. The point is that this ad didn't just say "no cholesterol." It said no cholesterol, *so don't worry*. Relax. Go nuts. Pig out, in other words. Eat all you want.

The ad raises the issue of sensible eating, then deflates it, strongly implying that mixed nuts provide no cause for dietary concern. Which is disgraceful, misleading, and fundamentally dishonest—because, as any physician will tell you, going nuts on salted nuts is nuts.

By the way, that "good stuff" from the label? This is the list in its entirety: vitamin A, 0 percent (of the recommended daily value); vitamin C, 0 percent; calcium, 4 percent; iron, 8 percent; phosphorus, 10 percent; magnesium, 15 percent; copper, 20 percent. Oh, yeah, that'll give Centrum a run for its money.

Here's another infuriating example: a 1983 campaign for Campbell's soups titled "Soup Is Good Food," one of the more extravagant episodes of using small facts to tell the Big Lie in advertising history. Now, look here: Campbell's soups aren't poison. They're warm and yummy and somewhat nourishing. They are also, however, loaded with sodium, placing them way high up on the watch lists of the food police. And if they don't raise your blood pressure, the tactics of this campaign will.

Campbell's funded an involved study in the esoteric dietary-science category of "nutrient density." The idea is to look at a given food's nutrient content not in pure terms, the way it shows up in ingredient labels, but in ratio to calories the food contains. To cite one very obvious example, 100 calories worth of cola contains about 1 percent of the recommended daily allowance of calcium. But 100 calories of milk contains 30 percent of the recommended daily calcium allowance. Calorie for calorie, therefore, milk contains thirty times more calcium than cola. That's clear enough, comparing one obvious source of calcium to one obvious nonsource. But that's not what Campbell's did. Its ads contained facts such as this: "Calorie for calorie, Campbell's tomato soup has more vitamin C than carrots or apricots." That's technically true, leading consumers to the conclusion that Campbell's tomato soup is a prime source of vitamin C. As it happens, though, carrots and apricots, as a ratio to their calorie content, aren't themselves particularly vitamin C dense. They sound like they might be, but they aren't.

And neither is Campbell's soup. Rigging the specs this way, you could also observe that, calorie for calorie, mud is a better source of iron than orange juice. That's true, too. It's also dangerously misleading, because orange juice contains no iron—but drinking it provides the vitamin C required for the body to absorb iron from other dietary sources. And mud is mud. Thus can facts misrepresent truth, with the public's nutritional well-being hanging in the balance.

How could it be that advertisers behave at their worst when the stakes seem to be the highest? Is it not loathsome to position, say, granola cereals as some sort of cholesterol cure when they are laden with sugar and saturated fat? How can anyone justify lulling consumers into a false sense of balanced nutrition while selling them precisely the substances that they, for health reasons, wish to avoid? Sara Lee and Ben & Jerry can sell all the crap they wish; they aren't pretending to do any different. But to market junk food as health food is a perversity. Advertising can do no worse.

Oh, wait a minute. Yes it can. Because there's always the over-the-counter medicine category, after political advertising the sleaziest of them all. It is a genre that for decades has been systematically, and in my opinion intentionally, confusing consumers about what chemicals are being offered and what benefits those various chemicals confer.

Take the cold/flu/allergy segment. There are three common, chemically similar antihistamine drugs: diphenhydramine (Benadryl), chlorphenamine (Chlor-Trimeton), and tripolidine. They all relieve sneezing, itch, and watery eyes, but they all can cause severe drowsiness. There are two principal and closely related OTC decongestants: pseudoephedrine (Sudafed) and phenylpropanolamine. These relieve sinus congestion. And there are a handful of analgesics, chief among them acetaminophen (Tylenol), aspirin, and ibuprofen (Advil and Motrin). Those eight drugs—plus a couple of others treating coughs

—represent the entire universe of nonprescription cold and allergy medications. Contac, Comtrex, Dimetapp, and the other dozens of permutations on the store shelves all include some combination of these same pharmaceuticals.

"Sinus" formulas include one of the decongestants. "Nondrowsiness" formulas leave out the antihistamine. Headache relief? Throw in some acetaminophen. It's that simple—which is why the drug companies seek to make it seem so complex, so mystifying.

So proprietary.

For decades, the various marketers have methodically stated or implied special expertise, special benefits, superior relief when there are none whatsoever. No wonder. Otherwise consumers might buy antihistamines, decongestants, and analgesics à la carte and treat themselves according to their immediate symptoms. That the manufacturers' shameless behavior promotes overmedication and undermedication has always made such smoke and mirrors unforgivable. But it gets even worse than that. In 1999, McNeil Consumer Products Co. and Saatchi & Saatchi, New York, actually sought to undermine consumer confidence in an entire class of competing products. Not content to confuse the issue vis-à-vis other patent medicines, Tylenol Allergy Sinus began warning people to second-guess their physicians' prescriptions. The text:

"A lot of people think that the best way to deal with allergies is to take a prescription. A common misconception, because when it comes to all your allergy symptoms, Tylenol Allergy Sinus gives you more relief than even the leading allergy prescription. You see, the leading prescription only relieves these symptoms . . . ."

(Onscreen type: "Itchy Watery Eyes, Itchy Runny Nose, Sneezing.") "But Tylenol Allergy Sinus relieves all these" (more type: "nasal congestion, sinus pressure and pain, and headache."

Then the tag line: "Take comfort in our strength."

Here's a better idea. Take umbrage at their outrageous deceit.

What this ad fails to mention (it was still running as of this writing) is that the prescription antihistamines it refers to—Claritin and Allegra—treat allergy symptoms without drowsiness. Because of these revolutionary drugs, many patients no longer have to choose between debilitating hay fever and debilitating drowsiness. If a doctor prescribes Allegra and the patient also wants sinus and headache relief, the appropriate treatment is most likely to add a decongestant and analgesic as needed—not to substitute Tylenol Allergy Sinus, containing the OTC antihistamine and the sedative effect that comes with it.

To watch that ad is to wonder where the federal regulators to stop this train wreck-waiting-to-happen are. My guess is that they all took Tylenol Allergy Sinus and are asleep at the switch.

The main question is, though, why lie? It makes no difference whether the selling proposition is unique if that proposition is fundamentally misleading. Can the possibility of a transitory market advantage be worth the damage to advertising in general—and to your soul? Surely your blood boiled to read the perversion of truth promulgated by would-be legislator Mike Pocalyko. Please don't kid yourself that what Campbell's and Tylenol Allergy Sinus did is any different. No matter how accurate the constituent facts, and no matter how artful their arrangement, they all amount to deception. The people who trade in half-truths may see themselves as opportunistic marketers. They may think they're simply salesmen putting their best foot forward. They may even fancy themselves masters in the art of selective information. What they are is a bunch of liars.

Now, go back and look at those Gallup results. Do you suppose the industry is so widely loathed because people are fed up with letterbox formatting and sans serif headline fonts? Nobody wants to be taken for a liar. If you're in the business and wish to preserve your image and self-respect, you might consider not lying.

COME ON DOWN TO OUR
THOUSANDS DEAD SALE-A-BRATION!

Oh, and while you're working on not being taken for a liar, you might also try not being taken for money-grubbing, exploitive scum. You know, if you can spare the time.

I refer to the inability, by many marketers, to resist the temptation to boost their public images—and sales—on the backs of other people's calamities. Now, look, obviously, apart from conveying important news about goods and services, advertising's number-one job is to enhance the image of the advertiser. It's not just a question of wanting to serve consumers' needs; you also want them to like you. If you are in a parity category, and they like you more than they like the other guy, and your prices are the same, you're going to get the business. No argument there. What's astonishing, and very often nauseating, is the lengths advertisers will go to—usually futilely—to command respect.

Let me offer one modest example. (Not because it isn't itself flagrant, but because, compared to other ones, which will make the enamel peel off your teeth, it is merely disgraceful.)

It ran in 1996, a five-minute documentary-style commercial, gray and grainy, opening with a vista of New York Harbor. A dramatic shot of the Statue of Liberty gives way, thanks to a depth-of-field shift, to an urban tangle of utility poles and phone wires obscuring the lady's heroic visage. We are in the mean streets of Jersey City, New Jersey.

"Once upon a time," says the voice-over, "before the budget cuts and the deficit, there were places where being a kid was no harder than climbing a set of monkey bars. This is the story of what happened when a group of people decided that once upon a time was too long ago."

Thus began the infomercial from Hal Riney & Partners, San Francisco, for Saturn Corp., documenting the construction of thousands of dollars worth of playground equipment in twelve sites around New York. The film recorded the cheerful efforts of Saturn volunteers amid the bleak realities of the inner city. "Now this is what Saturn's all about," says Chairman Skip LeFauve, clad in a T-shirt and jeans, taking a break from his labors. "Saturn's more than a car. I mean it's always been more than a car. This is sort of an expression of what our philosophy's all about."

Oh, really?

The genius behind Saturn marketing from the beginning has been Riney's ability to portray Saturn ownership not as the purchase of sheet metal but as entry into a community—a community of other Saturn owners, of dealership employees and assembly-line workers all with a stake in the neighborly, unpretentious Saturn ideal. Not since the Volkswagen Beetle has a car advertiser so successfully cultivated an image of self-effacement and quiet dignity. So it seems natural for Saturn retailers to venture into their local communities and foster in real ways the values expressed in the advertising. And, of course, it is natural for a company so committed to hope someone notices. The history of corporate charity is to manage, as discreetly as possible within the bounds of taste and propriety, to let as many people as possible know how selfless and caring you are. That means you can call your facility for families of cancer-stricken children Ronald McDonald House.

It doesn't mean you slap a sign on the Golden Arches reading "2 million sick kids' parents served."

The distinction apparently eluded Saturn. For what the company spent to dispatch its executives to New Jersey, and to film the construction, it could have built a dozen more playgrounds. For what it spent to air the spot, it could have built a different kind of playground, in every different kind of state of the union. So much for quiet philanthropy.

At one point in the spot, retailer Jorge Rodriguez shared an observation about the location, which was not exactly a neighborhood that generated a lot of sales for him. "We said, 'Yeah, this may not be the best PR place, but this is the right place.'" Well, Jorge, no problem. The economic hardships of the neighborhood aren't too limiting when you're broadcasting your munificence clear across the country. In fact, you *need* the economic hardships of the neighborhood, don't you? Or you'd have no heroic story ostentatiously to tell.

Sure, Saturn helped those depressed communities. Saturn also exploited those depressed communities, shamelessly exploited them—and all of the cinematically documented ethnic beneficiaries of the corporate largesse.

Helpful hint: If you brag about it, it ain't charity. It's promotion, with poster children.

Still, on the advertising vulgarometer, Saturn's exercise in self-congratulation was nothing. While the devastation of the inner city certainly is tragic, it also is chronic, lacking the emotional potential of acute catastrophe. To really cash in on the misfortunes of others, you've really got to have your large-scale conflagration, your disaster, your sudden death. Such as the 1995 Oklahoma City bombing.

Whenever tragedy strikes, a familiar passage from Ecclesiastes is quoted again and again: "A time to be born, and a time to die . . . A time to kill and a time to heal; a time to break down, and a time to build up . . . a time to mourn, and a time to dance; A time to cast away stones, and a time to gather stones together. . . ." The verse is timelessly eloquent and too often chillingly appropriate, but just as often it has been cut short, depriving us of one of its most trenchant admonitions: "a time to keep silence, and a time to speak."

Would that it had been called to the attention of Makita power tools. A few days after 168 men, women, and children were murdered at the Alfred P. Murrah Federal Building, Makita invested

$57,500 in a full-page ad in *USA Today*, the open letter headlined "OUR HEARTS ARE WITH YOU:"

"Today, hundreds of courageous rescue workers are putting their own safety at risk in hope of bringing the Oklahoma City tragedy to a conclusion. Makita Power Tools are with them in spirit and *on the rescue site*. To these dedicated professionals and the untold numbers of volunteers—on behalf of Makita USA, Inc., our employees, and the thousands of retailers who market our power tools and equipment—we ask that you accept our heartfelt appreciation. Your selfless courage in the face of this unparalleled disaster is an inspiration to us all. Our hearts are with you."

The letter was signed by Noriyasu Hattori, Makita's president.

The "on the rescue site" emphasis is mine. The grotesque indecency was Hattori's.

So Makita tools were on-site in Oklahoma City. Big freakin' deal. The manufacturers of yellow police tape didn't feel the need to weigh in. How about the nice folks at California Professional Manufacturing Inc., Modesto, makers of fourteen styles of quality body bags for more than a decade? No, they didn't either. Inasmuch as bomber Timothy McVeigh's cowardice left a smoldering tomb, a city in mourning, and a nation in shock, who the hell cared what brand power tools were being used? Nobody, and that's exactly the way it should have stayed. The ad may have said, "Our hearts are with you." What readers could not have failed to take from it is: "Makita tools: Powerful enough for the Oklahoma City rescuers, powerful enough for you!"

It's as if Hattori went to a stranger's funeral and—upon paying his respects to the bereaved family—fell to his knees sobbing, focusing all attention on himself. Actually, it's worse than that. It's as if he sobbed and quaked so uncontrollably that other mourners rushed to comfort him, whereupon he presented them with his business card.

But there's even worse. Much worse.

In 1998, in the midst of the Kosovo war, the Philip Morris Co. dispatched a planeload of food—estimated by the *Wall Street Journal* to have a wholesale value of $125,000—to a refugee camp in Albania. Crates of Kraft Macaroni & Cheese perhaps did not make a vast difference in the human suffering caused by Serbian genocide, but it helped, and it was vastly appreciated. The shipment fed thousands of Kosovars, young and old, who might otherwise have gone hungry. And there to document the operation was Philip Morris public-relations executive Molly Walsh.

A few months later, though, the big money started to flow. Philip Morris, through its agency Leo Burnett, spent approximately $1 million to stage and film "Molly's Story," a re-creation of the airlift, filmed in the Czech Republic, with an actress playing Molly and 350 extras dressed as desperate Kosovars. Then the company spent an undisclosed number of *tens of millions of dollars* airing the epic, sixty-second tale of corporate generosity.

Because at Philip Morris, they care.

The stinking, preening jackals.

This horrific display of twisted values was, briefly, the most perverse insult to genuine humanitarianism in American advertising history. Then came September 11.

Forgive me, once again, for quoting myself, but I call your attention to my first column after the terrorist attacks. After cautioning Madison Avenue about innocuous humor that might suddenly appear tasteless, I recalled the egregious excesses of Makita and Philip Morris and offered this: "Advertising must resist a parallel temptation to pin a black ribbon to its sleeve. The most insensitive punch line, on the continuum of shamelessness, has nothing on the ad that wraps itself in the mantle of patriotic fervor or ostentatious grief. This is no time for bathos. . . . National suffering and brand building have nothing to do with one another, and never should. Not only is it contemptible to exploit the grief of a nation to turn attention on one's corporate self, such grandstanding trivializes the very human tragedy it seeks to exploit."

I may as well have lectured to a wall. Within a few days thousands of advertisers, large and small, were trading in the free market of anger and grief. Most of the messages were earnest. Many of them were poignant. Others awkward and off-putting but well intended nonetheless. All over the world, including the corporate world, people were overcome by the enormity of the horror, giving rise to dual feelings of helplessness and purposefulness. Saying something was as close to doing something as they could get, so, like so many of us, they wore their emotions on their sleeves.

Hyperventilated speech isn't necessarily the consequence of small-mindedness or chauvinism or hypocrisy. Sometimes an abundance of feeling simply overwhelms or, shall we say, transcends the limits of language. Love of country is difficult to articulate without sounding simplistic or banal. What love isn't?

Whether statements of the obvious add much to the discussion is a legitimate question. The satirical newspaper the *Onion* certainly explored that line of inquiry with a story hilariously headlined, "Dinty Moore Breaks Its Long Silence on Terrorism." But if individuals draw comfort at a time like this by grasping the hand of the body politic, there's no reason corporations can't, too. At such moments of national coalescence, the lip service that companies typically pay to their "communities" of customers and suppliers, and even competitors, actually becomes true.

Sure, I guess I snickered at the sign outside the Rehoboth Beach, Delaware, bait shop ("God Bless America. Fresh Mullet") and rolled my eyes over Cox Cable's determination to express its corporate feelings on Channel 2 twenty-four hours a day. Even when the two-bit opportunists and profiteers crawled out of the woodwork, I didn't know whether to laugh or cry: spam-marketed offers for such indispensable trinkets as "Top Quality 24-Karat Goldtone Brass Christmas Ornaments" from Executive Industries in Las Vegas ("Celebrate the Holiday Season & Show Your Support for Our Great Country!") and special enrollment opportunities from the health-club chain New York Sports Club under the banner "Keep America Strong."

But then came General Motors.

"On Sept. 11," one ad from McCann-Erickson, Troy, Michigan, began, "the world as we knew it came to a halt. We sat glued to our televisions, watching events unfold that shook us to our very core. And, suddenly, the little things that had previously divided us became wholly insignificant. Now, it's time to move forward."

The commercial went on to announce—because what's good for GM is good for America—interest-free financing on every new GM car or truck. The company would have been using some sort of rebate or consumer incentive at that stage anyway, as it routinely does during auto-sales slumps. But here was an opportunity to position its givebacks not as corporate panic but as a solemn patriotic duty. Our patriotic duty, evidently, was to buy an Impala. "This may very well be the most serious crisis our nation has ever faced. In this time of terrible adversity, let's stand together. And keep America rolling."

Yes, the fabulous October Three-Thousand-Dead Sale-a-Bration.

Ford Motor Co., via J. Walter Thompson, Detroit, was right there on its heels with "Ford Drives America," which asked us to applaud its generosity and self-sacrifice. "In light of these challenging times, we at Ford want to do our part to help move America forward."

Repulsive. Simply repulsive. While it is true that our political leaders encouraged us to get back out into the economy, to pervert that message into a self-serving sales promotion was a cynical exploitation of the terrorists' victims and an unforgivable insult to those who grieve for them. No matter what the automakers claimed about preserving jobs and keeping the economy moving (effects that would be clearly proven transitory with a corresponding, time-delayed slump in first-quarter auto sales), the invocation of national interest here was a pretext, a transparent gimmick to convert a nation's inchoate emotions into year-end deliveries. Furthermore, it was utterly unnecessary. They could have merely announced zero-interest financing and sung its praises to the heavens. Offer it and they will come. But, no, why be simply compelling when you can play on the emotions of a traumatized society and fashion yourself a corporate hero? What does simple human decency have to do with it? You are General Motors. You are Ford. The sacred burial grounds of September 11 are yours to trample, hoisting the flag, desecrating the victims, for the holy purpose of moving the merchandise. The terrorists strike. You conquer. My God, will there ever be a reckoning?

WIN-WIN AND WE ALL LOSE

One last thing: cause-related marketing.

Marketers love it. Charities love it. I hate it.

This is something I've always felt, but also always wrestled with, because I'm not too stupid to see the evident "win-win" allure. If a company can build sales by pledging a portion of its profits to charity, and if the charity benefits from large donations it would likely otherwise never receive, where's the harm? It would seem to be a reasonable way to analyze the question. Then I met Jared.

Jared, radiant in the thirty-second TV spot from D'Arcy Masius Benton & Bowles, Chicago, is a sweet little boy whose jug ears and big-tooth smile seem all the bigger with his hair just now growing back in. He is at the moment full of energy, full of life, splashing and frolicking in a Florida swimming pool. He is also, officially, terminal.

"I went to Sea World and I saw the dolphins," he says, like any ten-year-old, stiffly narrating footage of what he did during his summer vacation. "I made lots of friends. I went swimming every day. I'm a great swimmer."

God bless Jared and his high spirits in the face of mortality. God bless his family. And God bless Give Kids the World, the wonderful charity that provides their free week in Orlando. God bless them, and heaven help us all, for when the voice-over offer begins, we realize that this is no mere advertising tearjerker. It is the main element of the big Procter & Gamble summer diaper promotion.

"Every time you buy Pampers in July," says the voice-over, "a portion of your purchase will be donated to Give Kids the World, a charity that gives kids like Jared and his family a week at their village near Orlando, because laughter really is the best medicine."

Then we see happy Jared again, and what is there to do but gasp?

Not because the cause isn't worthwhile; Give Kids the World is not only doing heroic work but is the rare charity that spends only 5 percent of its budget on administrative costs and every other nickel on its mission. It depends on corporate donations for 90 percent of its revenue.

And not because the advertiser lacks compassion. P&G and its employees generously devote time, resources, and more than $1 million to this and other charities. The issue isn't whether P&G's corporate heart is in the right place. The issue is whether this commercial and this promotion are unseemly, manipulative, and disgraceful.

And the answer is: of course they are, because this ad exploits the tragedy of Jared and his family. Because its inherent bathos exploits the emotions of the viewers. Because using images of a terminally ill child to get a spike in diaper sales is unspeakably perverse, no matter who benefits.

What it comes down to—and this is why I no longer wrestle with the question—is that cause-related marketing isn't philanthropy at all; it is a licensing agreement, a promotional tie-in. Only instead of *Shrek* or *Star Wars*, the tie-ins are with rain forests and hunger and dying children. And that isn't right. It is wrong.

Back when the Jared promotion ran, I spoke to the director of Give Kids the World, who said if I would only visit Orlando and see the joy her program brings, I'd understand why cause-related marketing is so wonderful. Sure, I said. But first I asked her if she would send Jared door to door, selling diapers to solicit funds. She said of course not. It would be degrading and unthinkable.

Yes, and in the summer of 1999, televised.

BLESS ME, GARFIELD, FOR I HAVE SCREWED UP BIG TIME

So, at my daughter's high school, there's a very active chapter of DECA, which is sort of the Junior Achievement of marketing, advertising, and PR. Naturally, when the adult sponsors realized a prophet was in their midst, they asked me to lend support—specifically, to help vet student teams' big annual projects. And, naturally, because I am a solid citizen who buys local produce and separates recyclables, I readily agreed.

My job was to read an elaborate, thirty-page documentation of the students' semester project on discouraging teen smoking and to sit through the presentation they would be making at the international DECA conference. This I did. Then I gave them my honest evaluation.

Now, perhaps you're thinking, No. No, no. He would never do to high-schoolers what he does to grown-ups. He would never do *that*.

Well, you would be thinking wrong. I eviscerated the little brats, whose written report—while undeniably impressive—was riddled with spelling and grammar errors, wordy and pompous phrasing, and dubious data analysis. My thinking was that the other adults would patronizingly tell them, "Hey, kids, darn nifty job!" and then the kids would go to the competition and get niftily trounced.* So, in as encouraging a tone as I could muster, and with all the proper pre-ambular congratulations for the sophistication of the project and the immensity of their effort, I sliced them open and removed their lit-tle teenaged spleens.

Constructively, of course.

When the bloodletting was over, two of the three youngsters mouthed boilerplate expressions of gratitude (although, truth be told, they both looked positively stricken). The third, who looked fazed not at all, cheerfully looked me in the eye. "I have a question for you," she said.

"Yes, sweetheart," I replied, "shoot."

"Have you ever been in advertising, or do you just write about it?"

It was technically a question, so I favored her with a reply: "I've never been in advertising a day in my life."

"That's what I thought," she said. And just the slightest smirk crossed her face, because, as far as this child was concerned, it was case closed. I'm just a Monday-morning quarterback, so how could I possibly presume to be giving advice to in-the-trenches DECA prac-titioners, much less actual advertising professionals?

Suffice it to say the thought was not unique to her. I get it all the time, all over the world. By now, you, the reader, having been graced by the holy beneficence of my words, understand how silly the question is. Bela Karolyi never performed on the uneven paral-

---

*One month later, the Robinson High School DECA Chapter took top international honors in Salt Lake City, Utah, for its antismoking project.

lel bars. Pauline Kael never directed a movie. Dr. Joyce Brothers was never a professional boxer, but she managed, way back when, to answer the $64,000 question on the subject. Whether I've worked in advertising is not relevant to whether I understand it. Duh.

However, just to be on the safe side—and to satisfy all skeptical DECAns—I thought the least I could do would be to consult a few fellows who have plied the trade, to see if by any chance their real-world experience might echo anything I've been saying for the past two hundred pages. But I didn't want just anyone. They had to be brand names. In fact, not just brand names but category leaders, guys whose faces one day will be carved into advertising's Mount Rushmore. And they had to be willing to tell me the dumbest thing they've ever done in the business.

Yes, the dumbest. Their triumphs you already know about. Graciously and humbly, three such titans agreed to do just that. So, with no further ado: the confessions of some ad men:

Jeff Goodby, On Greed, Self-Delusion, and the Client's New Clothes

A founding partner of Goodby, Silverstein & Partners, San Francisco, Jeff Goodby left Hal Riney & Partners in 1983 to create one of the most celebrated shops of the era. Before that he worked at Ogilvy & Mather and J. Walter Thompson. Before that he was a newspaper reporter, and before that he went to Harvard, if you please. As a copywriter, director, and creative executive, he has amassed virtually every advertising award out there, including the Cannes Grand Prix. Among his most famous campaigns have been ones for Nike, Pacific Bell, the Oakland Athletics baseball team, Isuzu, E*Trade, and the California Milk Processors Board ("got milk?"). The partners sold

their agency to Omnicom in 1991, yet, as of this writing, though
filthy rich and awash in adulation, they were still at the top of their
game. Goodby spoke about an assignment his agency had from Nike
in 1998 for a premium line of sports apparel and accessories called
"The Alpha Project."

Goodby: The Alpha Project. Yeah, the thing that makes it really
interesting is it happened at a time when Nike had totally lost
confidence in itself. And, of course, Nike was all about confidence, you know? So losing it and going out and doing this
Alpha Project thing was like, we thought, implicitly an admis-
sion that you were in trouble.

Nike was a brand whose notoriety depended upon not
ever cracking that armor, never being in trouble and always
being incredibly cool under fire and just in front of everybody,
and never admitting that you had to try that hard to get
anybody's attention, because you were just too cool to have to
do that. And here they were sort of explicitly inventing a
brand to fix their brand. It was like a Nike Black Label or
something, and we thought that it was like giving up on the
main brand. Maybe it was a good idea to create a Black
Label, but in a way it was going to devalue the whole rest of
their idea. So that's why, I think, we fought it for as long as
we did.

But eventually—and this is probably the object lesson to
this thing—when this starts to happen, everyone loses their
perspective, and so there's nobody in the room anymore who
has any connection to the truth or the real world or any kind
of common sense. And suddenly things that would make no
sense to a schoolboy are being seriously talked about by
heavy-duty marketing people who are about to spend millions
of dollars on them. And that's what started happening.

The makes-no-sense-to-a-schoolboy chapter set in, and we were right in the middle of it. We were in the middle of the swirling winds of nonsensicalness.

I mean, the really interesting thing was we said to them, "OK, well, let's make believe that this is a good idea to have this sort of Black Label special Nike superbrand, uberbrand. What are the products that are going to impress us like this?" This is a running joke in our office: They would say, "Well, we have a watch."

We go, "OK. A nice little digital watch, yeah? You say, it's a running watch? OK, what else you got?"

"Well, that's all we've got right now."

"Well, you're going to have to get some more things. You're going to have to have some shoes and, you know, they're going to have to be amazing products."

And they said, "Well, we don't really have amazing products. We're just kind of hoping that we could promise the amazing products and they'd sort of follow eventually."

And then they showed us the logo designs for it, which Silverstein had a coronary about, because they were too complicated and difficult to work with, and then we were laying that on top of the regular Nike logo. And so he was pretty much apoplectic after that. And so we set out to do the advertising for it, and I think we did—gee, it must have been six or eight rounds of lots of different campaigns. Again and again and again, going back and forth.

I think that the real reason that they didn't buy them wasn't that they weren't good. It was a combination of two things: It was that there was no product to make you go "Wow, this is really special, so it's going to work." And the other thing was it was implicitly, I think, a repudiation of the main brand. Kind of hidden in there is this embarrassment about the main brand. And so nobody wants to buy commercials that seem to implicitly repudiate your main brand, especially after you've worked at this place that is extremely aware of employee loyalty. You know, it's a very "drink the Kool-Aid" kind of place. It didn't sit well with them. You could see. I think that's why it took so many different rounds of advertising until finally, I think, we did ads that were essentially about nothing. There was nothing there. We ended up doing things like commercials about a goat boy that made very little sense except that shoe we were advertising looked a little bit like—it had a sort of cloven-hoof look to it. There was another commercial in which NBA star Gary Payton goes into some pawnbroker's shop and buys another head or something.

Me: With all sorts of grotesque special effects that involved, if I'm not mistaken, some sort of decapitation.

Goodby: Yeah, and in print ads that included spectacular Photoshop creations, you know like people playing tennis with fireproof suits on and stuff. But the product itself was nothing. It was like a shirt that was supposed to enable you to remain cooler while you were playing tennis—which they already make. They already had done years of advertising for products like that. So there was nothing new to the product, and there was nothing worthy of this much fanfare, yet we went out and got Michael Bay, you know, the director of *Pearl Harbor* and, especially pertinently, *Armageddon*. You know, he'd be the logical guy—the movies in which, you know, forces from beyond attack you. The whole thing was an enormous flop, financially and certainly in a marketing sense. I think it was off the air as soon as it was on. But the products, no one was ever going to buy these products at these prices for whatever reason. And I think that they dodged the bullet by having the thing disappear as quickly as it did. And, as I say, if there is any Alpha left, it's certainly not being portrayed as their Black Label brand. As far as I know, most of the Alpha products have ended up being turned back into regular Nike products or sold on eBay. Like: "actual, original Alpha shoe."

Me: OK, at the risk of sounding impertinent, and far be it from me to accuse you of glossing over really the critical point here, but your client approaches you with an assignment that you are philosophically and on grounds of pure common sense opposed to . . .

Goodby: Why didn't we say, "Absolutely not. We won't do it." Is that what you mean?

Me: Yeah.

Goodby: Well, I think it would have had greater implications. I think that first of all, I guess at some level, yeah, we were being mercenary and trying to hold on to the entirety of the account by allowing a mistake to be made in what we thought was a smallish sector to begin with. But it began to grow, you know, in this cancerous way. I think that as that happened, as I said, we all lost perspective on it. I think we started to convince ourselves that the advertising wasn't that bad and that it wouldn't matter that the products were really not that breakthrough. Yeah, I think there was a certain amount of compromise that we began the process with, but it was kind of lost in the machinations of the process, unfortunately.

Me: So it is like taking the SATs, where they tell you, if you're not certain, to stick with your first answer?

Goodby: Yeah, exactly. That's exactly what it's like—except that it was a world where you just lost track of what your first answer was. You had erased it so many times you couldn't tell which dot was your original answer.

Me: And in the end you lost the business.

Goodby: I think that, as much as anything, this Alpha Project probably was the thing that killed the relationship because . . . after this whole thing a lot of the people up there left, and I think they were tarred with this brush. And marketing people came in who hadn't been on Alpha, and they did what marketing people often do, which is go "Oh, my God, how could they possibly have done that? Let's find everyone who did it and get rid of them." And I think we were kind of part of that purge because I think they were appalled by the whole mechanisms of Alpha and how it happened. Not that they stood up and said, "That works sucks. You guys are fired." But I think that it made them lose confidence in the marketing people up there and, hence, in us, and so on. And it made them really feel like they had to have this cleansing kind of return to a one-agency system and so on.

So it had bigger implications than just the end of that one project. I mean, we had done wonderful advertising for them, extremely successful particularly on the women's World Cup soccer team. It was an incredibly big success. And that skate boarding scene that won the Grand Prix at Cannes and a girls' basketball campaign where we invented this team in Tennessee and sort of went to an imaginary season with them—all these things. And a wonderful print campaign, sort of empowering teenage girls to be more cynical about the way that magazines portrayed them and the whole idea of beauty and the public eye. I think we had done a lot of really magnificent work for them. Not to be obnoxious, but this thing was such a disaster that I think it just pushed the reset button on all that shit.

Me: Well, thank you. Now I'm going to make a one-time offer, which you have to act on instantly, because after that it goes away.

Goodby: OK.

Me: A "'drink-the-Kool-Aid' kind of place?"

Goodby: You can use it.

Dan Wieden, On Trying to Reinvent the Wheel

Dan Wieden (pronounced WHY-den) cofounded Wieden & Kennedy (pronounced KEN-edy) in 1982 as an oasis for those who believe that the creative product comes before everything else. Of course, most agencies are founded with approximately that vision, and within about five minutes the mission statement is balled up and trashed on the way to a new-business pitch for Appleby's or some such. Astonishingly, Wieden & Kennedy has remained true to its founding vision. Sure, it's done some dreadful work (Diet Coke comes to mind), but mainly it has performed with rare virtuosity, forsaking growth and acquisition lucre for quality and independence. Among the results are brilliant campaigns for Miller High Life beer, ESPN SportsCenter, and, above all, Nike. "Just Do It" is probably the most successful and historically significant campaign since the introduction of the Marlboro cowboy, the rare advertising that not only promotes the brand benefit but is part and parcel of it.

On the other hand, in 1991, there was the Subaru account . . .

Me: OK, what did you do wrong, when did you do it, and how?

Wieden: I suppose that it begins with the eternal optimism of a young agency looking at a car account, which is an enormous opportunity, with a lot of money and a lot of advertising dollars, so your work gets seen. Good chance to grow up. And grow up we did. I don't think we realized quite how much this was a little puppy chasing a steam engine. I think what we didn't appreciate, and I don't think the client really appreciated, was the depth of the issues they were facing as a business and our total lack of experience and that they probably needed a much more traditional agency with a lot more car experience to pull them out of the box that they were in. The two years we had the business we had three presidents of Subaru, you know. I mean they were in a lot of turmoil.

Me: Which led to bad advertising decisions?

Wieden: I think probably our initial attack on the thing was improper, which was "this is a car for people who basically don't give a shit about cars." It's something that gets you from point A to point B and is extremely trustworthy, but there's no real glitz or glamour or anything like that. It's not a status symbol; it's for practical people. Which, in fact, was for the kind of folks who were buying Subaru. That basic positioning of the car to its existing audience wasn't really inspirational for accruing new customers to the Subaru franchise, whatsoever.

Me: Although that strategy—cultivating known users—did work for Volkswagen a few years later.

Wieden: Yeah . . .

Me: What else?

Wieden: Well, it was our first office outside of Portland—I guess we had an office in Amsterdam, which ran pretty well independently—but I think probably there was not enough connection between Portland, myself most notably, and the office in Philly, near the client's south Jersey headquarters. I just kind of assumed it would run by itself, and they needed a whole lot of backup that they didn't get from me. And my brother gave me fair warning when we got the piece of business. Ken had worked on Saturn at Hal Riney & Partners. He was creative director on Saturn, and when he heard that we had picked up Subaru, he said, "I just need to tell you one thing: you do not have one client, you have 750 clients, and they're called dealers." And I don't think we really prepared properly for the decentralized nature of a car account, especially one where the president is changing as frequently as they did on Subaru.

At the National Automobile Dealers Association meeting, they actually had a voodoo doll of me in a booth, with pins sticking in it. That's how bad it was. Yeah, the lessons we learned were enormous. I think what happened is when the relationship started going wobbly, the work did not improve; it got worse. It seemed like we did not know who to please and we kept trying to please everybody or else to say "Screw them; we're just going to do something we like," and neither one of those things worked.

Me: I want to ask you about one of the last ads in the campaign, featuring a skinny little jerk talking about corporate rock and roll . . .

Wieden: Oh, wow, I'm not remembering . . .

Me: This is the skinny little Gen-X actor talking about Moses Malone, I think, about crashing backboards and punk rock versus "corporate" music and that's why Subaru is the right wagon for you. Do you remember this?

Wieden: No . . . You see? Any man worth his salt has some means of blocking memories that are so painful.

Me: That's when I wanted to come through the TV screen, and, you know, tiptoe on the electrons like the stones in a river and strangle you.

Wieden: Well, you were not alone. That's where you get in this trouble, where you assume that if you show the customer his own face he'll immediately embrace you in some sort of insightful brand. It was quite awful actually.

Me: What was your life like in those days?

Wieden: Oh, it was high anxiety. I mean Subaru accounted for so much of our business, and we had a whole office full of people there that were devoted to it and to that alone, basically. So, losing that piece of business was like sawing off one of your appendages, so you fought to keep it, tried to keep it even though it was just tearing the organization up.

Me: Was there some single mistake of yours? Do you go back to some moment that seems like the thing that you opened the wrong door to? Had you made a different decision, listened to some cautionary voice in your head, listened to your brother . . .

Wieden: Well, I don't think so. It was a little bit more like falling into quicksand, you know. You think, "Oh, it's not so bad. All I need to do is get over there to the edge and we'll be fine." So the very struggle to get over there just makes you sink deeper into it, you know. I don't think it was like hitting a trip wire. It was more subtle and more insidious than that. And I think that's true of most problematic accounts. You get them, and they always start off with a great deal of excitement, and things are going to be wonderful, and then you start seeing signs that "Oh, wow, this is more difficult than we thought." And it usually is an indication that you and the client are in two different universes and never the twain will meet.

I don't want to throw too many insults or accusations at Subaru, because I think we need to just acknowledge what we did wrong, and they clearly were able to right that ship and sell a lot of cars. I think probably one of the other main things we did is, we never actually told them that they ought to focus on that little wagon and just fund that son of a gun. You had a lot of dealers who said four-wheel drive doesn't make any sense in the South; we don't have that snow and ice problem. So you had a political situation that seemed to be impossible. And instead of us being very blunt about what they needed to do and give them the kind of advice they probably needed to hear whether they wanted to or not, we probably were way too polite and tried to be accommodating.

Me: All right, so now you're giving advice, you're passing on all of your knowledge to your son or your figurative son. You put your arm around the boy and you say, "Son . . . "

Wieden: Well, if you're entering into a new category, it might not be the best idea in the world to pick up the fallen and wounded. You probably will have a better shot at succeeding if you've got a company with a good product and with some upward momentum, rather than the reverse. And, in any event, you need to make a combination of really experienced people and pull them together on this business as well as some folks that are new to the business. I think that combination is really important. If you just throw experienced people at it, you just keep making the same appeals that have been made for centuries, and they're not necessarily that interesting. And if you just use new folks, you make the kind of mistakes we did.

Me: What was the low point? What was the point where you wanted to sort of curl up in the fetal position and just cry?

Wieden: Well, I think the low point, actually, was when it was over and we had a contract with them, which meant we had to continue servicing the business for several months afterward. So that meant we had to keep the office open and let people go in stages, which was unbelievably painful. I came in one day, and I guess like half the office was still there, and one of the women that we had had to let go early was there with her baby; she'd been on maternity leave. And she was showing the baby off to some of the women in the office, and I walked by and I was standing there, and the baby threw up, and the mother turned to me and said, "That was for you, Dan."

Me: What did you say to her?

Wieden: Not a thing. Not a thing.

Phil Dusenberry, On Being Blinded by Your Own Brilliance

Phil Dusenberry retired in mid-2002 after a brief, forty-year stint with BBDO. His title when he retired was chairman, BBDO, North

America. But his business card easily could have read "Phil Dusen-
berry, Man in Whose Image a Gigantic Worldwide Agency Has
Evolved." Whether the client is Visa or FedEx or Snickers or Camp-
bell's Soup, there is a distinctive BBDO look, and Phil Dusenberry
created it. The most characteristic expressions of his oeuvre are long-
standing campaigns for General Electric and Pepsi-Cola, but the
same combination of production slickness and naked emotion were
also evident in his work for Ronald Reagan's ad hoc Tuesday Team,
which invited the electorate to ignore the economic reverses of the
president's first term and bask in the renewal of "Morning in
America." Dusenberry also famously wrote the screenplay for The
Natural, *based on Bernard Malamud's novel about a deeply flawed*
baseball slugger. In the book, faced with one last opportunity for
redemption, the dying star strikes out. In the movie, Robert Redford
hits an electrifying home run, triggering gooey sentiment and screen
pyrotechnics. A big hit, in other words, yielding a big hit. But of
course it was. Again and again over four decades in advertising,
Dusenberry caught lightning in a bottle and optimism, dramatically
photographed, on film.

Me: You've had a long and varied and heroic career, but
somewhere along the way you must have done something
that, to this day, makes you shudder or cringe or wince. What
is it?

Dusenberry: Probably the one that makes me wince more than
the others was the campaign we did in '98 for Pepsi. It was
called "GeneratioNext." That was the theme of it. And what
we were trying to do, we were trying to be supercool to the
audience. We were talking to a very young audience. But in
trying to do that we became really sort of *un*cool, because we
were too narrowly focused on teens, and we totally blew it.
We didn't appeal to a broad range of users, and, actually, we

alienated a ton of Pepsi drinkers by trying to be too cool, too hip, too much inside to the teenage market. As a result we ended up with a campaign that really fell flat on its face. We showed it to the bottlers in Hawaii, and it played to gales of silence. And, while there was one spot out of it that rang the bell (it became, in fact, the number-one spot in the Super Bowl in the Ad Meter poll, a commercial called "Goose," where a guy is flying and a goose flies up next to him and takes a drink of his Pepsi), the rest of the pool was really a complete flop, and it was one of the worst moments in my career and all of us who worked on Pepsi at the time. It just shows what happens when you try to be a little too hip, a little too contemporary, a little too smart for your audience, when in fact you are just absolutely going right past them.

Me: What were some of the other spots in that pool?

Dusenberry: One of the other spots in the campaign was a spot called "Gnat." It was an animated bug sucking Pepsi, a drop of Pepsi, from a bar counter, and then he starts dancing and singing to the Rolling Stones' "Brown Sugar." There was another spot, which I kind of liked, but it was just absolutely, you know, nobody could get with it. It was a commercial called "Pierced." It never actually saw much airtime. It was terribly received at the bottlers' convention. There's a guy, a young guy, at an outdoor concert, who is drinking Pepsi, and he then spurts from the piercings all over his face. In other words, as he's drinking the Pepsi, the little piercings on his face actually start spurting little streams of Pepsi. People were just turned off by it. And, you know, we thought kids would like it, find it to be a really hip spot, but we totally missed the mark.

Me: So, you show these spots to the bottlers, and they sit there in a deafening silence; they're clearly not amused.

Dusenberry: Right.

Me: Was there no warning voice that was sounded along the way, either in your head or explicitly from people who watched the process along the way who said, "You know, maybe we're going down the wrong path here?"

Dusenberry: Well, sometimes when a group of people work on a creative project together, it becomes a little inbred. Everybody sort of begins thinking alike. And that's fine, except that you sometimes lose your objectivity and you lose your focus. Everybody, including our clients, was part of this team, and we were thinking that we were really going to ring the bell with kids, with teenagers. Unfortunately Roger Enrico, then PepsiCo CEO, never got to see the work until he was sitting in the audience that night with those bottlers. And he of course said later on that if he had seen this work he never would have allowed it to have been shown. So, to answer your question, the answer is no, we just went blindly along thinking we had this thing really nailed, and no one came and said, "Wait a second; this stuff just isn't right." That some-times happens.

Me: Well, you'll be interested in my Chapter 8. It goes into this very phenomenon you're describing. So, what was it like sitting in that audience? I mean were you squirming?

Dusenberry: It was terrible. I was standing up in the back, and it was a huge audience. I'm talking thousands of people. And, I could just sense the undercurrent of disenchantment; you could just feel it, that, sort of, rumble of disgruntlement, and you knew, uh-oh, this is going to be a long night, and it was. The next day Roger called us to his hotel room in Kauai and read us the Riot Act and said, "You guys better get this thing back on track, because we've got a real disaster here." So we did. We managed to come back within a very short time, and one of the things we came back with was the little girl, you know, the little gal, Hallie . . .

Me: Eisenberg.

Dusenberry: Yeah. That of course turned the whole thing completely around. But for that interim period we knew that this was going to be a tough row to hoe, and we had to really get back on track here.

Me: How was that eleven-hour flight from Honolulu to New York?

Dusenberry: It was pretty awful. It was a pretty awful flight. In fact, midway through that flight I literally got sick and had to get off the plane and spend the night in San Francisco. I just wasn't feeling well at all. I don't know whether that was just a coincidence or part of the aftermath of that terrible convention.

Me: There's this phenomenon when the fifteen-year-olds are having the party, and Dad materializes at the bottom of the steps wearing baggy shorts and unlaced high-top basketball shoes. Is there any greater pain in the world for the fifteen-year-old than watching his dad try to be young like him? Is that what was wrong with those spots?

Dusenberry: Not really. I mean, yeah, I know what you're saying. The older guy is trying to act young. It wasn't that so much as that the spots themselves were too hip for their own good. And, in fact, here's the interesting punch line: these spots actually did well overseas; not in America, but in Europe, where the audiences there, the teenagers there, are a little bit more advanced in some ways and are more receptive to things that are a little further off the wall. It had a much greater acceptance there. But it wasn't like it was just old graying guys trying to act young. It was really just, I would say it's a moving target, and we missed. And, it was just too narrowly focused. And, as a result, we lost a lot of the upbeat inclusive spirit and tone of this historical Pepsi advertising. The best advertising we've always done for Pepsi has always been advertising aimed at young-thinking people, but always somehow had an appeal to older folks as well. I can't explain it exactly. It would be like the kind of commercial that people would look at who are older and say, "Look, I know that's not for me, but, you know, I enjoy watching that." And, that's what these missed. I mean these just absolutely had no appeal to anyone beyond the teen years, and even to that audience they missed as well. Our best stuff has always had a universal appeal even thought it's aimed at and skewed to a younger audience.

Me: So, what's the Pepsi commercial that you regard as your greatest single triumph?

Dusenberry: I think, perhaps, the best Pepsi spot we ever did—I didn't do it myself; I was involved as creative director in the business at the time—was a commercial called "Sound Truck." It was a young kid in a little van who sets up an audio system where we begin to hear the sounds of a Pepsi being opened on a beach through an amplification system. I don't know if you remember this spot.

Me: I remember it vividly.

Dusenberry: Yeah. And it began to whet people's appetite for whatever it was. And the kid finally opens up the back of his truck and puts on his Pepsi hat, and he says, "OK, who's first?" And by now thousands have gathered outside his van. It was a simple spot, because it had appetite appeal, it had youth appeal, it had thirst appeal; it had so many great things going for it that I felt it was the best spot that we had ever done, against many different measures. It was one of my all-time favorites.

Me: And was the process for creating that spot any different than for creating the campaign that was such a disaster in Hawaii?

Dusenberry: Actually, the process was not really different, and it was the same people, which is an interesting thing: the same people worked on both projects. I mean, Ted Sann wrote the spot I just described, and Ted also worked on the 1998 debacle. So I guess it just goes to show you can't hit a home run every time out.

Me: Does it go to show you anything else?

Dusenberry: Well, it shows you that it's good to take a reality check. That sometimes you can—I think that there was a turning point in our relationship with Pepsi and our relationship even among ourselves—that you can't be right all the time, and, you know, the chances are you might be wrong and you better take a reality check, and you'd better say, "Hey, wait a second; is this the right thing to do?" We've done that much more ever since that happened. I'm not saying we're looking over our shoulder or whistling in the dark, but the reality check is much more a part of what we're doing now than it was then.

GO FORTH AND ADVERTISE

I f Newton Minow was right about television's "vast wasteland"—
and, oh, lordy, was he ever—whatever are we to conclude about
the ads that, like so many sun-bleached cattle skulls, for half a century have littered the desolate horizon?

Just think of the most indicting examples. The relentless,
headache-inducing petulance of the Ted Bates Agency's Anacin commercials. ("I'd rather do it myself!") The grotesque, smirking sexism
of the old National Airlines' "Fly me!" campaign, in which the slogan—uttered by foxy stewardesses—was a vulgar double entendre.
The carcinogenic cunning of Joe Camel. The trick-little-kids dishonesty of Hot Wheels. Grim remnants, one and all.

Then there was the casual racism of the Frito Bandito, the prey-
on-suckers sleazism of the Psychic Friends Network, and the per-
verted grocery squeezism of Mr. Whipple. We can never forget how
they treated us—i.e., like idiots and fools. Nor can we forget the sor-
did history of shameless appeals to our vanity, materialism, sexual
baseness, and shallow obsession with status—to say nothing of inces-

sant tugs at our neurotic insecurities about such planetary scourges as halitosis, dishwasher spots, nasty heel marks, and static cling.

And, post-traumatic stress disorder being what it is, we can never fully rid our memories—God help us all—of Madge.

"You're soaking in it!" she shrieked, for about twenty years.

Yo, Madge, you cackling harpie, go to hell.

Go to hell for being the apotheosis of human irritation—fingernails on the blackboard at sixty cycles per second—and go to hell especially for being right. We're not merely exposed to TV advertising; we're soaking in it. Factor in the dubious—or, at least, unquantifiable—effectiveness of the entire discipline and its overarching incitement to mindless consumption, and one can easily see how what my magazine called the "Advertising Century" can be written off as a sorry display of capitalist excess, a toxic by-product of the Information Age.

"You realize," says the anarchist Canadian magazine *Adbusters*, "that all the hoopla obscures one very dirty little fact about our consumer culture: it thrives on the death of nature and charges the cost to future generations."

To critics such as these, advertising must be understood in ultra-macroeconomic terms, wherein every transaction is judged not by its contribution to the gross domestic product—and certainly not by its comfort or value to the individual consumer—but by its ultimate cost to the environment. To them, television commercials are the moral equivalent of napalm—which means, I suppose, that Tony the Tiger is an enemy of the people. Any way you shake it, theirs is a sobering condemnation of an industry and a way of life.

It's also ludicrous.

Advertising is many things. Unadulterated evil is not one of them. From the singing Texaco men on, television ads have benefited society in many ways. Indeed, there is ample reason not merely to abide the accumulation of Madison Avenue's output but to cherish it. Let's start with one benefit wholly unintended by anyone involved: anthropology. There may be no richer archive for the social and cultural historians of our age than the aggregation of a half-century's advertising.

"These humbler adjuncts to literature may prove more valuable to the future historian than the editorial contents," wrote early adman Elmo Calkins, as quoted by Martin Mayer in *Whatever Happened to Madison Avenue?* "In them we may trace our sociological history, the rise and fall of fads and crazes, changing interests and changing tastes in food and clothes, amusements and vices, a panorama of life as it was lived, more informing than old diaries and crumbling tombstones."

If advertising were nothing else, it would be valuable as the Rosetta stone of the consumer society. To trace the evolution of women in American life, for instance, an anthropologist could find no more availing source than a year-by-year compendium of laundry-soap and packaged-foods commercials. I'm thinking, say, of the spot for Whip 'n Chill, in which a stern husband recalled, "Last week I laid down the law: no more of those tea-party desserts." Cowed by his ultimatum, the little woman bought the advertised brand, which was light but also rich and satisfying, staving off divorce or spousal abuse. Then there was poor Mary Jones, the robotic hausfrau depicted going back and forth from the kitchen in comical quick motion, yet still disappointing her nerdy husband with the same boring old entrees. But when she served him Chef Boy-ar-dee Goulash, suddenly his sense of romance awakened and his sexuality was aroused. Soon they were cheek to cheek in a tempestuous Hungarian dance. What happened next was left to the viewer's imagination, but it certainly wasn't Whip 'n Chill.

Another delight starred Fred MacMurray, the sinister film noir villain–turned–emasculated widower on TV's "My Three Sons." In a spot for Chevrolet, he encountered a ditzy housewife at a loss to locate the tailgate to her Chevy station wagon. Playing off her obtuseness, MacMurray reeled off a list of product features, including the wagon's smooth ride. The lady, ever confused—because she was a woman and therefore incapable of grasping technical concepts, such as driving—confirmed his thesis with her experience: "I never know when I run over the garden tools!"

Such condescending vignettes were undeniably guilty of placing women in submissive, or at least subservient, household roles. And when you show them to women today you may actually see steam shooting, cartoonlike, from their ears. But what better artifacts of another time and place? It's not as though there was some sinister conspiracy of male ad execs scheming to subordinate women in the male-dominated society. These ads, from a certain moment in our history, all were the result of consumer research that reflected— for better or worse—prevailing attitudes, especially among the women in the target audience. Women *did* do all the cooking, sew on the buttons, do the dishes, schlep the kids, and they *did* care deeply about how well they performed these roles. It was that caring that was reflected in the ads. The stereotype may be egregious—Fred MacMurray, who was nobody's image of an intellectual—talks to the ditzy lady as if she were six years old. And, yes, such advertising did perpetuate such values and attitudes. But it didn't invent them. And the advertising survives to document where we were and how far we've come.

The service of scholarship, obviously, is a subsidiary benefit. Let us not neglect advertising's principal one: the small detail that it has helped move trillions of dollars in merchandise. I have spent time over the past nine chapters railing about how oblivious, and occasionally hostile, ad practitioners can be to their fundamental purpose. But not always. First of all, advertising works. Even bad advertising works in the rudimentary role of reinforcing a brand name and of conveying the presumption of quality and substance conferred by the mere existence of national advertising. Further-more, much advertising is simply brilliant, building brands, culti-vating markets, and creating wealth that serves not only this country's economy but that of the entire world. What Michael Jordan and "Just Do It" did for Nike, what "Mo-naaaa" did for Gillette Right Guard, and (alas) what Mr. Whipple did for Charmin toilet paper is incalculable—which is to say both enormous and impossible to quantify.

Curiously, the very incalculability that certifies advertising's vast achievements also seems to provoke the industry's harshest critics, who take positions on opposite poles of the continuum of contempt.

To those who see hidden psychological persuaders lurking behind every still image and frame of film, and who believe George Lois's fatuous boast that advertising is "poison gas," achievements in selling are by no means a badge of honor. They see TV commercials as casting some sort of Svengali spell, mesmerizing us into obediently buying all manner of goods and services we neither truly want nor need. This belief is the province of many a paranoiac crackpot—the sort who imagine pictures of genitalia embedded in ice cubes—but also by some canny and trenchant observers of the advertising scene. One such is Leslie Savan, ad critic for the *Village Voice*, who sees her role as informing readers what is behind TV commercials so they can be better prepared to repel the spots' sinister powers.

To Savan, commercials not only manipulate us; they do noth-ing less than compromise our humanity. In her 1994 collection *The Sponsored Life*, she cites William James's wistful contemplation of "liberation from material attachments, the unbribed soul" as her point of departure for her exploration of spiritual corruption—i.e., adver-tising's knack for both validating and perpetuating unrealistic notions of human fulfillment, their exhortation to derive meaning from things instead of ideas. The disturbing consequence is what she calls "a uniquely American form of spiritual graft."

The assumption is that any deviation from ascetic devotion to the inner life is an unacceptable compromise, that any material indulgence is essentially corrupt. If you follow the sentiment to its logical conclusion, central heating is bribery of the soul and a microwave oven is naked hedonism.

Now, Savan is no Buddhist monk, or Taliban mullah, and she is no crackpot, and she obviously does not prescribe a merchandise-free society. So she would have to agree that to appreciate certain material things is not necessarily to worship them. Consumption—tuberculosis imagery notwithstanding—is not in and of itself a disease of the soul. Nor is the advertising that seems to stimulate it—at least not now that Calvin Klein has calmed down.

The flip side of the thirty-second Svengali is the equally skeptical, equally extreme argument that tens of thousands of TV commercials, year in and year out, have scarcely worked at all. This view is proffered by my friend Randall Rothenberg in his book *Where the Suckers Moon*, which takes delight in attributing the sales-explosion phenomena of Nike and Volkswagen, for example, to prevailing economic and social conditions—as opposed to Wieden & Kennedy's and Doyle Dane Bernbach's brilliant, classic advertising. The campaigns were swell, Randy says, but mainly these were just two marketers in the right place at the right time.

Whatever. Advertising's fundamental efficacy isn't really at issue. The incontrovertible proof lies in the fact that when ad campaigns cease, sales always go down. Period. Once again, putting aside qualitative differences among campaigns, advertising contributes an aura of substance and dependability on national brands, and therefore actually represents some of the value we demand from products we trust. That the mechanism behind this process is mystifying takes nothing away from the phenomenon itself.

That, of course, is the minimum effect of advertising. When everything is going just right—"Where's the Beef?" for instance—the brand can transcend the marketing nuts and bolts of its category and vault headlong into the national psyche. Not to mention extraordinary riches.

In the ordinary course of events, the effect of advertising falls smack between Vance Packard's *The Hidden Persuaders* and Randy Rothenberg's scenario of extraneousness; it influences our buying decisions but by no means dictates them. For every "Where's the beef?" deployment of poison gas there is a benign bicarbonate like Alka-Seltzer, which provided campaign after delightful, memorable, hilarious campaign and lost market share the entire way.

Still in all, as Martin Mayer put it, "What advertising does reverberates beyond the statistics." Such as, for example, bankrolling television, radio, newspapers, magazines, and in large part the Internet. In that sense Minow had it exactly right, but Marshall McLuhan had it slightly wrong. The medium isn't the message. The medium is *brought to you* by the message.

Maybe at some rarefied, solipsistic, theoretical level the meaning of the TV signal derives from the very presence of the TV signal, but the real impact of TV is in the particulars. Uncle Miltie. The Army-McCarthy hearings. The Cuban missile crisis. "Laugh-In." The Tet offensive. Archie Bunker. The moon landing. The fall of the Berlin Wall. The death of Princess Di. "Survivor." The collapse of the Twin Towers. Each set of images was in its own way a watershed, each leaving an indelible imprint on society. And each paid for, directly or indirectly, by the sponsor. Whatever else can be debated about the advertising age, this is undeniable: it has underwritten the revolution.

Fire. The wheel. The printing press. The steam engine. Antibiotics. The integrated circuit. Digitization. TV is on the short list of innovations that changed humankind, and this one was on Madge's dime. Indeed, one can posit a powerful argument that the TV signal—and both the programming and advertising it carried—changed the world in a quite specific way by substantially undermining the Communist bloc. The Iron Curtain could keep people in, but it couldn't keep the news of the consumer society out. When, through broadcast and video, people in the East realized what was being advertised and purchased in the West, the fraud of Marxist rhetoric was at last all too evident. Without glibly ignoring the impact of President Reagan's "Star Wars" bankrupting the Soviet command economy, and the ultimate moral bankruptcy of communism itself, it's reasonable to view the collapse of the Soviet empire as simple neighborhood dynamics of the global village: keeping up with the Joneses on a grand scale.

Then, of course, lest we forget, there are the ads themselves. The history of TV advertising is by no means simply the decades' accumulation of waxy buildup. Madge notwithstanding, it's not just a rogues' gallery of irritants. It's also a pantheon of triumphs.

Let's begin with the noncommercial ones, because, yes, that great moral compromiser, that sinister Svengali, that destroyer of the rain forest has often been a potent force for social welfare. Of the images burned forever in the mass consciousness, so many are from public service announcements written, produced, and donated for the greater good. Among them: Smokey the Bear, the fried-egg image of "Your Brain on Drugs" and Iron Eyes Cody, the crying American Indian, heartbroken over the ravaging of the environment. Then there was the sixties classic "Like father, like son," which depicted an adoring little boy mimicking his dad's every move. The last image is of the father lighting a cigarette—among the most powerful invitations to epiphany ever filmed.

More recently, in 1992, there was the public service announcement for the New York Coalition for the Homeless that shows nothing more complicated than a montage of street people in their various wretched habitats, singing "New York, New York." But in its simplicity resided its astonishing power. First, the lyrics tumbled with devastating irony from the mouths of society's detritus. "I want to wake up in the city that doesn't sleep/be king of the hill, top of the heap"—this from a man whose shelter was on a heap of trash. Grim irony aside, however, what really registered was how these woeful men and women, reduced to the brutal indignity of homelessness, effortlessly sang the song.

After viewing that spot, it may still be possible to be irritated by the homeless, to fear them, to resent them, but it is impossible to succumb to the temptation of denying them their humanity. It is impossible to forget that these people are indeed people—people who know the words and melodies to pop tunes, just like us. On such wonders must advertising also be judged.

F. Scott Fitzgerald, the immortal economist and moral pillar, wrote that "Advertising's contribution to humanity is exactly minus zero." Pity he drank himself to death before TV came of age.

It isn't just Madge and Whipple that the ad industry has wrought. It's George Raft leading a prison dining-hall disturbance, a young groom trying to digest the idea of poached oysters or "Atsa some spicy meatball!" for Alka-Seltzer. It's Joe Isuzu and "Joey called," via AT&T, just to say I love you. It's "I'd like to teach the world to sing in perfect harmony"; the Pepsi Generation; and "Wouldn't you like to be a Pepper, too?" It's the 7UP "uncola nut" and the fast-talking man for Federal Express. It's Mean Joe Greene with a smile and a jersey for a little kid, and it's a lonesome snowplow operator driving to work in a Volkswagen Beetle. It's Bill Denby joining a pickup game of hoops, prosthetic legs or no. It's Arthur Godfrey prattling on, with his unique combination of sincerity and irreverence, looking for the chicken bits in the Lipton chicken noodle soup. Yes, indeed. It's where's the chicken, and it's "Where's the beef?"

Vast though the wasteland may be, the way to understand and benefit from it is not to survey its emptiness. The trick is to mine its precious, sometimes hidden treasures. To say only that advertising has informed our language, our culture, our economy, and our democracy is to circle the periphery. The central truth is something greater. In the end we must acknowledge that advertising—with all that it has wrought—is one of the things that makes us us.

So, if you happen to be employed in the advertising industry in any capacity, and if you should happen to find yourself occasionally brushing your teeth in the morning, staring at your mirrored image glumly because your livelihood depends on moving, say, an extra thousand boxcars full of toilet paper, and you feel like a parasite or disappointment or a traitor to your ideals, get over it. You are engaged in a perfectly honorable profession. After all, you could just as easily be a real parasite—a criminal, or a real estate agent or an anchor on Fox News Channel.

Yet in my twenty-year association with the advertising community, I have often been struck by its sense of institutional self-loathing. Probably I mentioned this earlier. In fact, surely I mentioned this earlier, because I always mention it. I stop strangers on the street to mention it, because it explains a great deal. In creative departments it seems there is hardly a soul who wouldn't prefer to be painting paintings or directing films or doing stand-up comedy or just about anything besides flogging toilet paper and patent medicines and who-knows-what-all for businessmen clients they neither like nor understand. As we saw in an earlier chapter, this hostility creates a creative tension that every now and then yields genius but mostly just gets in the way of the job.

That's so unnecessary, because advertising clearly has an intrinsic value all of its own. And while it may not be art, it is certainly an art form, worthy of engagement and mastery. Why fight advertising for what it isn't when it is so much more productive to embrace it for what it uniquely is?

So go forth, my children, and advertise. Seek the true and righteous path. Nurture the holy alliance between art and commerce and plant the fecund seed of thine imagination deep into the fertile soil of the economy. Thou hast nothing to be ashamed of. As somebody once said, just do it.

But, for God's sake, do it my way.

AFTERWORD

This ad criticism thing wasn't my idea. I was sort of dragooned into service, because Barbara Lippert, over at our competition, was beating our brains in with her marvelous column. So, thanks first to Barbara. Thanks second to two *Ad Age* editors: Fred Danzig and my dear friend (and sometimes infuriating nemesis), the late Dennis Chase, who did the dragooning. Thanks third to former managing editor Val Mackie, who forced the "Ad Review" star system down my throat like corn into a goose.

You don't just walk into a newsroom and immediately vault into the upper middle of business journalism. This takes the support of many colleagues, beginning with my friend J. Taylor Buckley, who greeted me on my first day at USA Today, six weeks before that paper's debut in 1982, with the news that I'd be writing the advertising column. It seemed like a stupid idea at the time, but Taylor's a visionary. Clay Felker, the legendary magazine editor, also is a visionary. I solicited his advice in 1985 before joining Ad Age, and he told me I was out of my mind. He was right, but I took the job anyway.

At Ad Age I have worked with a remarkable series of editors: Fred, Dennis, Steve Yahn, David Klein, and my pal Scott "Scott" Donaton, all of whom have been unstinting in their support of "Ad Review." This support derives naturally from the editorial philosophy of Ad Age's founder, the late G. D. Crain, that journalism drives the business, not vice versa. His legacy lives through his sons, Keith and Rance, who run the company with a nearly fanatical devotion to editorial independence. Rance hired me in 1985, and though he agrees with me only 38.4 percent of the time (because he is wrong 61.6 percent of the time), he has never put an ounce of pressure on me or altered a comma in my copy. Nor has anyone who works for him. Which accounts for the misspellings and fact errors.

Ha! Kidding! I've had immeasurable help over the years from managing editors Rick Gordon, Val Mackie, Melanie Rigney, Larry Edwards, and especially Judann Pollack, who so has me pegged. Saving my sorry butt more times than I count have been copyeditors Dan Lippe, Julie Johnson, Mike Ryan, Rich Skews, Julie Steenhuysen, Deborah Aho, Char Kosek, Gregg Runburg, Kim Narisetti, Ken Wheaton, Elaine Rocchi, and Sheila Dougherty. In various capacities and at countless times, I've been buoyed by current and former Ad Age big shots Larry Doherty, Bob Goldsborough, Joe Cappo, Anthony Vagnoni, and John Wolfe, my good friend and insufferable nuisance. As for Elizabeth Sturdivant and Shannon O'Boyle (who was especially tireless in researching examples for this book), they know I cannot function without them.

A quick word about the Side of Evil: as a matter of survival, I long ago decided not to mix with the people in the industry I criticize. But obviously I must be in regular contact with the advertising agencies that create the work I review. My liaisons are those agencies' PR executives, who as a group are the most cooperative, responsive, and astonishingly good-natured humans on earth. I can't possibly name everybody, but my sincere appreciation for years of consideration goes to all of them. Thanks especially to Judy Torello, Wally Petersen, Susan Irwin, Brad Lynch, Pat Sloan, Mary Churchill, Philippe Krakowsky, Jeremy Miller, Roy Elvove, Cheri Carpenter, Owen Dougherty, Michael Draznin, Liz Hartge, Amy Hoffar, Diane Iovenitti, Toni Lee, Jay Leipzig, Vonda LePage, Toni Maloney, Dorothy Marcus, Melanie Mitchem, Janet Northen, Elizabeth Reilly, Tom Robbins, Kathleen Ruane, Stacy Rubis, Nora Slattery, Jan Sneed, Lisa Wells, and the late, beloved Lou Tripodi. Without their cheerful efforts—often in the face of certain corporate catastrophe—my job would be impossible.

Likewise, let me express my endless gratitude to a roster of Advertising Age reporters even more too numerous to list who have been heroically cooperative over the years while taking most of the lumps from infuriated sources too chicken to berate me personally. It has been a privilege working alongside them.

This book would never have been possible without the persistence of literary agent Cynthia Manson and the support of Ad Age publisher Jill Manee. My book editor, Danielle Egan-Miller, has demonstrated unerring judgment, intellectual rigor, and amazing good humor in dealing with her cranky author. My extraordinary and inspiring wife, Milena Trobozic, not only insisted that I take on this project but vetted its contents and reduced herself to much degrading menial labor while I used the book as an excuse to evade husbandly responsibility, such as child care. And showering.

Special thanks to former vice president Al Gore for inventing the Internet, without which this volume never would have seen the light of day.

INDEX